THE BOOK OF
HOT AND SPICY
AND INDIAN FOODS

THE BOOK OF
HOT AND SPICY
AND INDIAN FOODS

TED SMART

Specially produced for Ted Smart,
Guardian House, Borough Road,
Godalming, Surrey GU7 2AE

ISBN 1 85613 034 7

This edition © Salamander Books Ltd., 1991

Recipes and photographs on the following pages
are the copyright of Merehurst Press:
3, Bottom and Right, 5, 6, 7, 8, 9, 10, 11, 12, 13, 14, 15, 16, 17,
18, 19, 20, 21, 22, 23, 24, 25, 26, 27, 28, 29, 30, 31, 32, 33, 34,
35, 36, 37, 38, 39, 40, 41, 42, 43, 44, 45, 46, 47, 48

All correspondence concerning the content of this volume
should be addressed to the publisher.

CREDITS

Designer: Sarah Cooper

Contributing authors: Linda Fraser, Louise Steele

Photographers: Paul Grater, Alister Thorpe

Typeset: Maron Graphics Ltd., Wembley., Walkergate Press Ltd., Hull

Colour separation: J. Film Process Ltd., Magnum Graphics Ltd.

Printed in Italy

HOT
AND SPICY

CHILLIES

Chillies belong to the pepper (capsicum) family, as do sweet peppers but there the relationship ends, for the fiery heat of the chilli is in no way similar to its mild-flavoured relation. Fresh chillies are now widely available and vary considerably in size, shape and heat factor. In principle, the fatter chillies tend to be more mild than the long, thin varieties, and the smaller the chilli, the hotter its taste. Generally, the unripened, green chilli is less fiery than when ripened and red, but there are exceptions according to the variety, so it is wise to remember that all chillies, irrespective of colour, shape and size, are hot, so use caution before adding them to a dish. Bear in mind that a little chilli goes a long way, so add a small amount to begin with and gradually increase the quantity to your liking during cooking.

Take care when preparing chillies – the tiny, cream-coloured seeds inside are the hottest part and, in general, are removed before using. Chillies contain a pungent oil which can cause an unpleasant burning sensation to eyes and skin, so it's a wise precaution to wear rubber gloves when handling chillies and to be sure not to touch your face or eyes during preparation. Cut off stalk end, then split open the pod and scrape out seeds, using a pointed knife. Discard the seeds. Rinse pods thoroughly under cold running water and pat dry before chopping or slicing as required. Once this task is completed, wash hands, utensils and surfaces with soapy water.

Dried red chillies are sold whole and can vary in size from 1-2 cm (½-¾ in) to 4-5 cm (1½-2 in) in length, so take this into account when using. If a recipe states small dried chillies, and you only have the larger ones, reduce the quantity accordingly. Dried chillies are usually soaked in hot water for 1 hour before draining and removing seeds (as described left), unless a recipe states otherwise.

Dried red chillies, when ground, are used to make cayenne pepper and, combined with other spices and seasonings, also make chilli and curry powder, and chilli seasoning. They are also used in the making of Tabasco and chilli sauce.

The Harissa spice mix, see page 8, uses a large quantity of dried chillies and is very hot, so be warned! This is a favourite spice mix for many Middle Eastern dishes. Don't be tempted to add more Harissa than recipe states, unless you are prepared for an extremely hot dish. A less fiery Harissa can be made simply by removing the seeds from soaked chillies, before crushing with other ingredients.

Green chillies are available canned in brine. These are often ready-seeded and peeled and taste pleasantly hot and spicy – ideal for adding to pizza toppings, sauces and taco fillings. Both red and green chillies also come pickled in jars (hot or mild/sweet) and can be found in specialist delicatessens and ethnic food shops. Canned and pickled varieties should be drained and patted dry before using. Whether you seed the pickled type is up to you, just remember the seeds are the hottest part!

MUSTARD

White or yellow, brown and black seeds all come from the mustard plant, according to the species. Most commonly found is the creamy yellow type (this is the one used to produce 'mustard and cress') which is the least pungent. The brown type (or Indian mustard) is stronger in flavour, while the black mustard seed is the most powerful of all. The creamy yellow seeds are more widely available, but look out for the black and brown types in Asian and Oriental food shops and specialist delicatessens.

Whole mustard seeds have a pleasant nutty bite to them and can be used to add piquancy to salad dressing and hot sauces – especially good when served with fish, chicken and pork. They are also delicious added to coleslaw and creamy potato salads and are a popular addition to pickles and chutneys. Use mustard seeds (especially the two hotter varieties) with discretion to begin with, increasing the amount as you become more familiar with the flavours.

It is the yellow seed, processed with black seeds, wheat flour and turmeric, which forms the basis of English mustard. Mustard powder can be used as it is in cooking, or may be mixed to a paste with a little cold or warm water. (For a richer mixture, it can be mixed with a little cream or milk). Once mixed it should be left for at least 10 minutes to allow time for the flavours to develop. It is only when the powder is mixed with a liquid that the essential oils are released, giving mustard its pungency and sensation of heat. Remember that made mustard loses its pungency after a few hours. Jars of prepared mustards, once opened, need using up within a few weeks as the flavour and colour will deteriorate.

The variety of ready-prepared mustards come in a bewildering number of mouthwatering flavours. These can be made from milled mustard flour, or from coarsely crushed seed (the proportions of which vary tremendously, depending on the type). Some are mixed with vinegar, others with grape juice or wine (and sometimes beer) and often contain various spices, herbs and seasonings, such as honey and horseradish. German mustard, which is mild and sweet-flavoured, is a mixture of brown and white mustard flour, moistened with vinegar and flavoured with various spices. The mild-flavoured American mustard (popular with children) generally uses only yellow mustard seeds with the addition of sugar, vinegar and salt. Dijon mustard, made from milled, dehusked black seeds, is flavoured with wine and spices. The pungent and spicy grainy types of mustard are a mixture of whole, crushed black and yellow seeds with additional flavourings added for individuality.

Mustards of all types can be used to great effect, not only as a condiment, but also as a culinary ingredient. They add bite and piquancy to all manner of savoury dishes from scrambled eggs, sauces and dressings, to devilled mixtures, barbecued foods, soups, casseroles, pastry or scones.

A–Z OF SPICES

Allspice (1) These small dark, reddish-brown berries are so called because their aroma and flavour resembles a combination of cinnamon, cloves and nutmeg. Use berries whole in marinades; for boiling and pot-roasting meats and poultry; in fish dishes, pickles and chutneys. Also available ground and excellent for flavouring milk puddings and cakes.

Anise (2) Commonly called aniseed, these small brown oval seeds have the sweet, pungent flavour of liquorice. Also available ground. Use seeds in stews and vegetable dishes, or scatter over loaves and rolls before baking. Try ground anise for flavouring fish dishes and pastries for fruit pies.

Caraway (3) Small, brown crescent-shaped seeds with a strong liquorice flavour and especially delicious as a flavouring in braised cabbage and sauerkraut recipes. Also in breads.

Cardamom (4) Small, triangular-shaped pods containing numerous small black seeds which have a warm, highly aromatic flavour. You can buy green or black cardamoms, although green are more widely available.

Cayenne (5) Orangey-red in colour, this ground pepper is extremely hot and pungent. Not to be confused with paprika, which, although related, is mild-flavoured.

Chilli powder (6) Made from dried red chillies. This red powder varies in flavour and hotness, from mild to hot. A less fiery type is found in chilli seasoning.

Cinnamon (7) and Cassia (8) Shavings of bark from the cinnamon tree are processed and curled to form cinnamon sticks. Also available in ground form. Spicy, fragrant and sweet, it is used widely in savoury and sweet dishes. Cassia (from the dried bark of the cassia tree) is similar, but less delicate in flavour.

Cloves (9) These dried, unopened flower buds give a warm aroma and pungency to foods, but should be used with care as the flavour can become overpowering. Whole cloves are added

to hams, soups, sauces and mulled drinks as well as stewed fruits and apple pies. Also available in ground form for adding to cakes and puddings.

Coriander (10) Available in seed and ground form. These tiny, pale brown seeds have a mild, spicy flavour with a slight orange peel fragrance. An essential spice in curry dishes, but also extremely good in many cake and biscuit recipes.

Cumin (11) Sold in seed or ground form. Cumin has a warm, pungent aromatic flavour and is used extensively to flavour curries and many Middle Eastern and Mexican dishes. Popular in Germany for flavouring sauerkraut and port dishes. Use in meat stews and stuffed vegetables.

Fenugreek (12) These small, yellow-brown seeds have a slight bitter flavour which, when added in small quantities, is very good in curries, chutneys and pickles, soups and fish dishes.

Ginger (13) Available in many forms. Invaluable for adding to many savoury and sweet dishes and for baking traditional favourites such as gingerbread and brandy snaps. Fresh root ginger looks like a knobbly stem. It should be peeled and finely chopped or sliced before use. Dried ginger root is very hard and light beige in colour. To release flavour it should be 'bruised' with a spoon or soaked in hot water before using. This dried type is more often used in pickling, jam making and preserving. Also available in ground form, preserved stem ginger and crystallized ginger.

Mace (14) and Nutmeg (15) Both found on same plant. The nutmeg is the inner kernel of the fruit. When ripe, the fruit splits open to reveal bright red arils which lie around the shell of the nutmeg – and once dried are known as mace blades. The flavour of both spices is very similar – warm, sweet and aromatic, although nutmeg is more delicate than mace. Both spices are also sold ground. Use with vegetables; sprinkled over egg dishes, milk puddings and custards; egg nogs and mulled drinks; or use as a flavouring in cake mixtures.

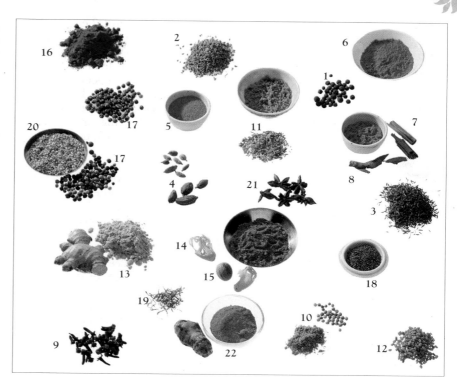

Paprika (16) Comes from a variety of pepper (capsicum) and although similar in colour to cayenne, this bright red powder has a mild flavour.

Pepper (17) White pepper comes from ripened berries with the outer husks removed. Black pepper comes from unripened berries dried until dark greenish black in colour. Black pepper is more subtle than white. Use white or black peppercorns in marinades and pickling, or freshly ground as a seasoning. Both white and black pepper are available ground. Green peppercorns are also unripe berries with a mild, light flavour. These are canned in brine or pickled, or freeze-dried in jars. They add a pleasant, light peppery flavour to sauces, pâtés and salad dressings. Drain those packed in liquid and use either whole or mash them lightly before using. Dry green peppercorns should be lightly crushed before using to help release flavour, unless otherwise stated in a recipe.

Poppy seeds (18) These tiny, slate-blue seeds add a nutty flavour to both sweet and savoury dishes.

Saffron (19) This spice comes from the stigmas of a species of crocus. It has a distinctive flavour and gives a rich

yellow colouring to dishes, however, it is also the most expensive spice. Available in small packets or jars (either powdered or in strands – the strands being far superior in flavour). This spice is a must for an authentic Paella or Cornish Saffron Cake. Also an extremely good flavouring for soups, fish and chicken dishes.

Sesame seeds (20) High in protein and mineral oil content, sesame seeds have a crisp texture and sweet, nutty flavour which combines well in curries, chicken, pork and fish dishes. Use to sprinkle over loaves, biscuits and pastries before baking.

Star Anise (21) This dried, star-shaped seed head has a pungent, aromatic smell, rather similar to fennel. Use very sparingly in stir-fry dishes; also good with fish and poultry.

Turmeric (22) Closely related to ginger, it is an aromatic root, which is dried and ground to produce a bright, orange/yellow powder. It has a rich, warm, distinctive smell and a delicate, aromatic flavour and helps give dishes an attractive yellow colouring. Use turmeric in curries; with fish and shellfish dishes; in rice pilaffs and lentil and other pulse mixtures.

SPICE MIXTURES

GARAM MASALA

10 green or 6 black cardamoms, pods cracked and seeds
  removed
1 tablespoon black peppercorns
2 teaspoons cumin seeds
½ teaspoon coriander seeds
2 small dried red chillies, seeds removed

Using a blender, grind all ingredients
together until finely ground. Store in an
airtight jar for up to 3 months. The amount of
spices used can be decreased or increased in
quantity, according to personal preference.

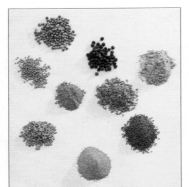

CURRY POWDER

2 tablespoons cumin seeds
2 tablespoons fenugreek
1½ teaspoons mustard seeds
1 tablespoon black peppercorns
8 tablespoons coriander seeds
1 tablespoon poppy seeds
1 tablespoon ground ginger
1½ teaspoons hot chilli powder
4 tablespoons ground turmeric

Using a blender, grind first 6 ingredients
finely. Add remaining ingredients and grind.
Store in airtight jar for up to 3 months.

FIVE-SPICE POWDER

5 teaspoons ground anise (aniseed)
5 teaspoons star anise
12.5 cm (5 in) cinnamon stick, or use the equivalent
  in cassia bark
6 teaspoons cloves
7 teaspoons fennel seeds

Using a blender, grind all ingredients
together until finely ground. Store in an
airtight jar for up to 3 months. This is a
favourite for Chinese dishes. It is strong-
flavoured, so should only be used in very
small quantities.

MIXED SPICE

1 cinnamon stick, broken into small pieces
2½ teaspoons allspice berries
3 teaspoons cloves
2 teaspoons freshly grated nutmeg
3 teaspoons ground ginger

Using a coffee grinder, or blender, grind
cinnamon, allspice berries and cloves
together until very finely ground. Add to
freshly grated nutmeg and ginger and mix
well. Store in a small, airtight jar for up to 1
month.

PICKLING SPICE

2 tablespoons mace blades
1 tablespoon allspice berries
1 tablespoon whole cloves
2 cinnamon sticks, broken into small pieces
12 black peppercorns
1 dried bay leaf, crumbled

Mix all ingredients together. Store in a small,
airtight jar for up to 2 months.

HARISSA

30 g (1 oz) dried red chillies
1 clove garlic, chopped
1 teaspoon caraway seeds
1 teaspoon cumin seeds
1 teaspoon coriander seeds
several pinches of salt
olive oil, to cover

Soak chillies in hot water for 1 hour. Drain
well. Pat dry and, using a pestle and mortar,
grind to a smooth paste with garlic, spices and
salt. Put into a small jar, add enough olive oil
to cover. Store, covered, for up to 2 months.

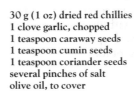

MARINATED OLIVES

125 g (4 oz/¾ cup) black olives
125 g (4 oz/¾ cup) pimento-stuffed olives
3 slices of lemon
3 dried red chillies
2 cloves garlic, crushed
1 teaspoon mustard seeds
1 teaspoon black peppercorns
3 allspice berries
about 315 ml (10 fl oz/1¾ cups) olive oil
lemon twists and sprigs of parsley, to garnish

Drain off any brine from olives. Put olives into a bowl.

Add lemon slices, chillies, garlic, mustard seeds, peppercorns and allspice berries. Stir in olive oil and mix well. Spoon mixture into a large jar (with a tight-fitting lid). Screw on lid tightly and turn jar over several times to ensure ingredients are well mixed.

Leave olives to marinate for at least 1 week before serving, turning jar several times a day. Serve as an appetiser with drinks, garnished with lemon twists and sprigs of parsley. (These olives can be kept for up to 6 months in a cool place.)

Serves 4-6.

Note: Use a mixture of corn oil and olive oil, for a more economical marinade. Add sprigs of dried herbs to the marinade, if desired.

BOMBAY NUT MIX

30 g (1 oz/⅔ cup) thin pretzel sticks
45 g (1½ oz/9 teaspoons) butter
1 clove garlic, crushed
60 g (2 oz/⅓ cup) unblanched almonds
60 g (2 oz/⅓ cup) pine nuts
60 g (2 oz/⅓ cup) unsalted cashews
1 teaspoon Worcestershire sauce
1 teaspoon Curry Powder, see page 8
½ teaspoon hot chilli powder
60 g (2 oz/⅓ cup) seedless raisins
¼ teaspoon salt

Break pretzels into 2.5 cm (1 in) sticks. Melt butter in a frying pan.

Add garlic to pan, then stir in almonds, pine nuts and cashews. Add Worcestershire sauce, curry powder and chilli powder and mix well. Stir in pretzels and cook gently over medium heat for 3-4 minutes, stirring frequently.

Remove pan from heat. Add raisins and salt and mix well. Turn mixture into a serving dish and leave to cool.

Serves 4-6.

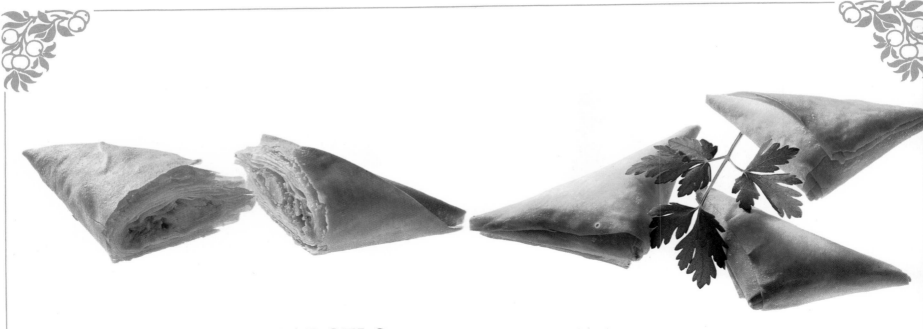

FILO PRAWN PARCELS

1 tablespoon sesame oil
2 tablespoons corn oil
1 clove garlic, crushed
1 onion, finely chopped
2.5 cm (1 in) fresh root ginger, peeled and grated
½ teaspoon turmeric
½ teaspoon chilli powder
¼ teaspoon ground cumin
185 g (6 oz) peeled raw prawns, thawed if frozen
30 g (1 oz/2 tablespoons) creamed coconut, diced
5 sheets filo pastry
60 g (2 oz/¼ cup) butter or ghee, melted
sprig of parsley, to garnish

Preheat oven to 180C (350F/Gas 4). Lightly grease a baking sheet. Heat sesame and corn oils in a saucepan. Add garlic, onion and ginger and fry gently for 5 minutes, stirring occasionally.

Add turmeric, chilli powder and cumin and fry gently for 2 minutes. Add prawns, then cover and cook gently for 5 minutes, stirring frequently. Remove from heat and stir in creamed coconut. Leave mixture to cool.

Work with 1-2 sheets of filo pastry at a time, keeping the rest covered with a damp cloth. Cut sheet of pastry in half lengthwise and then fold each piece in half lengthwise to give 2 long, narrow strips. Put a portion of prawn mixture in one corner of each strip of pastry. Brush pastry all over with a little of the melted butter or ghee.

Fold pastry and filling over at right angles to make a triangle and continue folding in this way along strip of pastry to form a neat triangular parcel. Brush all over with melted butter or ghee and put on greased baking sheet. Repeat this process with remaining sheets of pastry and prawn mixture, to make 10 parcels altogether.

Bake in oven for 20 minutes, then brush with remaining melted butter or ghee and return to oven for a further 5-10 minutes until parcels are golden brown. Serve warm, garnished with a sprig of parsley.

Makes 10.

TANGY POTTED CHEESE

125 g (4 oz/1 cup) finely grated mature Cheddar cheese
60 g (2 oz/¼ cup) butter, softened
3 teaspoons port or sherry
4 spring onions, finely chopped
½ teaspoon caraway seeds
½-1 teaspoon wholegrain mustard
¼ teaspoon Worcestershire sauce
30 g (1 oz/¼ cup) coarsely chopped walnuts
sprig of parsley, to garnish

Put grated cheese into a bowl and add softened butter. Mix well together until soft.

Stir in port or sherry, spring onions, caraway seeds, mustard and Worcestershire sauce and mix thoroughly until well combined.

Spoon mixture into a small dish, cover with chopped walnuts and press down lightly. Chill for at least 2 hours. Serve, garnished with parsley, with crackers or Melba toast.

Serves 4-6.

Note: This spread will keep in the refrigerator for up to 5 days.

Variation: Add 1 teaspoon chopped fresh herbs and a few pinches cayenne pepper to taste.

CHEESE CHILLI BITES

125 g (4 oz/1 cup) plain flour
¼ teaspoon salt
½ teaspoon dry mustard
¼-½ teaspoon hot chilli powder
large pinch of cayenne pepper
60g (2 oz/¼ cup) butter or margarine
60g (2 oz/½ cup) finely grated Cheddar cheese
1 egg, beaten
2 tablespoons sesame or poppy seeds

Preheat oven to 200C (400F/Gas 6). Sift flour, salt and spices into a bowl.

Rub in butter or margarine finely until mixture resembles breadcrumbs. Add grated cheese and mix well. Mix beaten egg with 1 tablespoon cold water. Add 2 tablespoons of egg mixture to bowl and mix to form a fairly stiff dough. Knead gently. Roll out dough on a lightly floured surface to a 15 x 30 cm (6 x 12 in) rectangle. Trim edges. Cut in half lengthwise and transfer to a baking sheet.

Brush each piece with remaining egg mixture and sprinkle with sesame or poppy seeds. Cut each piece into 10 triangular shapes and separate slightly to prevent them sticking together. Bake in oven for 10-12 minutes until lightly golden and cooked through. Cool on a wire rack.

Makes 20.

Note: Biscuits can be stored in an airtight container for up to 2 weeks.

CHICKEN LIVER PÂTÉ

MUSSEL SOUP

60g (2 oz/¾ cup) butter
1 onion, finely chopped
1 clove garlic, crushed
250 g (8 oz) chicken livers
1-2 teaspoons Curry Powder, see page 8
125 ml (4 fl oz/½ cup) chicken stock
2 hard-boiled eggs
salt and pepper
2 pinches of cayenne pepper
fresh bay leaves and lemon slices, to garnish

Melt half the butter in a frying pan. Add onion, garlic and chicken livers and cook gently for 5 minutes, stirring.

Add curry powder and cook for 1 minute, then add chicken stock and cook gently for 5 minutes, stirring and turning livers frequently. Put chicken liver mixture and hard-boiled eggs in a blender or food processor and blend to form a smooth purée.

Season with salt, pepper and cayenne pepper, then turn mixture into a small serving dish or terrine. Smooth the surface. Melt remaining butter in a pan and pour over surface of pâté. Leave to set slightly, then garnish with fresh bay leaves. Chill for several hours or overnight before adding lemon slices and serving with crusty bread.

Serves 6.

Note: Add a little curry powder to taste, to the melted butter topping, if desired.

1 kg (2 lb) mussels
315 ml (10 fl oz/1¼ cups) dry white wine
45 g (1½ oz/9 teaspoons) butter
1 tablespoon olive oil
1 onion, finely chopped
1 clove garlic, crushed
1 leek, trimmed and finely shredded
½ teaspoon fenugreek, finely crushed
1½ tablespoons plain flour
315 ml (10 fl oz/1¼ cups) chicken stock
two 0.05 g packets saffron strands, soaked
   in 1 tablespoon boiling water
1 tablespoon chopped fresh parsley
salt and pepper
2 tablespoons whipping cream
sprig of parsley, to garnish

Scrub mussels clean in several changes of fresh cold water and pull off beards. Discard any mussels that are cracked or do not close tightly when tapped. Put mussels into a large saucepan with wine and 375 ml (12 fl oz/1½ cups) water. Cover and cook over high heat, shaking pan frequently, for 6-7 minutes or until shells open. Remove mussels from liquor, discarding any which remain closed. Strain liquid through a fine sieve and reserve.

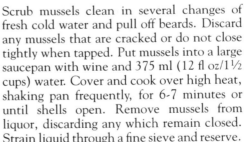

Heat butter and oil in a pan. Add onion, garlic, leek and fenugreek and cook gently for 5 minutes. Stir in flour and cook for 1 minute, then add 625 ml (20 fl oz/2½ cups) reserved cooking liquor, chicken stock and saffron mixture. Bring to boil, cover and simmer for 15 minutes. Meanwhile, keep 8 mussels in shells and remove remaining mussels from shells. Add all mussels to soup and stir in parsley, seasoning and cream. Heat for 2-3 minutes. Garnish with parsley and serve.

Serves 4.

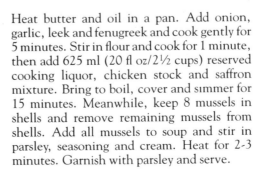

CHILLIED RED BEAN DIP

2 tablespoons corn oil
1 clove garlic, crushed
1 onion, finely chopped
1 fresh green chilli, seeded and finely chopped
1 teaspoon hot chilli powder
470 g (15 oz) can red kidney beans
60 g (2 oz/½ cup) grated mature Cheddar cheese
salt
thin slivers of fresh green and red chilli and sprig of
  parsley, to garnish
tortilla chips, to serve

Heat oil in a frying pan. Add garlic, onion, green chilli and chilli powder and cook gently for 4 minutes.

Drain kidney beans, reserving liquor. Reserve 3 tablespoons beans; purée the remainder in a blender or food processor. Add to pan and stir in 2 tablespoons reserved liquor and mix well.

Stir in grated cheese and reserved beans and cook gently for about 2 minutes, stirring until cheese melts. Season with salt and mix well. Turn into a serving dish and garnish with slivers of chilli and sprig of parsley. Serve warm, with tortilla chips.

Serves 4-6.

Note: If mixture becomes too thick, add a little more bean liquid.

SPICED MELON COCKTAIL

½ ripe Honeydew melon, seeded
155 ml (5 fl oz/⅔ cup) whipping cream
155 ml (5 fl oz/⅔ cup) mayonnaise
2 teaspoons lemon juice
1 teaspoon paprika
½ teaspoon Tabasco sauce
½ teaspoon Worcestershire sauce
2 tablespoons tomato purée (paste)
250 g (8 oz) white crabmeat, flaked
8 radicchio leaves, shredded
lemon and lime slices and sprig of mint, to garnish

Cut melon flesh into neat pieces, or scoop melon into balls, see Note.

In a bowl, whip cream until softly peaking. Mix in mayonnaise, lemon juice, paprika, Tabasco sauce, Worcestershire sauce and tomato purée (paste).

Stir crabmeat into dressing, then lightly mix in melon and toss ingredients gently until coated. Arrange shredded radicchio in 4 individual serving dishes and spoon the melon and crab mixture on top. Serve lightly chilled, garnished with lemon and lime slices and mint.

Serves 4.

Note: For melon balls, use a melon scoop and 1 ripe Honeydew melon (use left-over melon in a fruit salad).

DEVILLED TOMATOES

4 firm tomatoes
30 g (1 oz/6 teaspoons) butter
1 small clove garlic, crushed
30 g (1 oz/½ cup) fresh white breadcrumbs
1 tablespoon chopped fresh parsley
¼ teaspoon cayenne pepper
½ teaspoon paprika
½ teaspoon dry mustard
3 teaspoons grated Parmesan cheese
salt
sprigs of parsley, to garnish

Preheat oven to 180C (350F/Gas 4). Grease an ovenproof dish. Cut the top one-third off each tomato.

Reserve tops for 'lids'. Scoop out some of the seeds from each tomato. Arrange tomatoes, cut-sides up, in the dish. Melt butter in a saucepan. Add garlic, breadcrumbs and parsley and mix well together.

Remove from heat and add cayenne pepper, paprika, mustard and Parmesan cheese. Season with salt and mix well. Spoon onto tomatoes and form into neat mounds, pressing gently into shape with fingertips. Put reserved 'lids' on top. Bake in oven for 15 minutes. Serve hot, garnished with sprigs of parsley.

Serves 4.

ORIENTAL PRAWNS

8 raw Mediterranean (king) prawns
60 g (2 oz/½ cup) plain flour
¼ teaspoon salt
1 teaspoon corn oil
2.5 cm (1 in) piece fresh root ginger, peeled and grated
1 clove garlic, crushed
1 teaspoon chilli sauce
1 egg white
vegetable oil for frying
spring onion tassel and few strips of red pepper, to garnish

Peel prawns, leaving tail shells on. Make a small incision along the spines. Remove black spinal cords from prawns.

Put flour into a bowl. Add salt, oil and 60 ml (2 fl oz/¼ cup) water and mix together. Stir in ginger, garlic and chilli sauce and beat well. In a bowl, whisk egg white until stiff, then gently fold into batter until evenly combined.

Half-fill a deep fat pan or fryer with oil and heat to 190C (375F) or until a cube of day-old bread browns in 40 seconds. Hold each prawn by its tail and dip it into batter, then lower it into hot oil. Fry for 3 minutes until golden. Drain on absorbent kitchen paper. Serve hot, garnished with spring onion tassel and red pepper strips.

Serves 4.

CREOLE GUMBO POT

1 small aubergine (eggplant)
salt and pepper
3 tablespoons olive oil
1 large onion, chopped
1 red pepper (capsicum), seeded and diced
1 clove garlic, crushed
2 teaspoons paprika
½ teaspoon hot chilli powder
125 g (4 oz) okra
125 g (4 oz) frozen sweetcorn, thawed
470 ml (15 fl oz/2 cups) boiling chicken stock
250 g (8 oz) can tomatoes
30 g (1 oz/2 tablespoons) long-grain rice
250 g (8 oz) peeled prawns, thawed if frozen
sprig of dill, to garnish

Trim stalk end from aubergine (eggplant). Cut aubergine (eggplant) into 1 cm (½ in) pieces and put into a colander. Sprinkle with 2 teaspoons salt and leave on a plate to drain for 30 minutes. Rinse under cold water and drain well.

Heat oil in a saucepan. Add onion, red pepper (capsicum), garlic and aubergine (eggplant) and fry gently over low heat for 5 minutes, stirring frequently.

Stir in paprika and chilli powder and cook gently for 2 minutes. Trim stalk ends from okra and discard. Cut okra into quarters.

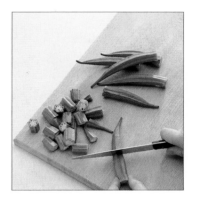

Add okra to pan together with sweetcorn, boiling chicken stock and the tomatoes. Break tomatoes up with a spoon. Stir in rice, then cover and simmer gently for 25 minutes until vegetables and rice are tender.

Add prawns to the mixture and heat through for 5 minutes, stirring occasionally. Taste and adjust seasoning if necessary with salt and pepper. Serve hot, garnished with dill.

Serves 4-6.

Variation: For a deliciously rich version, stir in 155 ml (5 fl oz/⅔ cup) single (light) cream just before serving and heat through gently.

FRIED CAMEMBERT

BARBECUED SPARE RIBS

four 45 g (1½ oz) portions fairly firm Camembert
2 teaspoons plain flour
½ teaspoon dry mustard
½ teaspoon dried mixed herbs
pepper
1 egg, beaten
30 g (1 oz/¼ cup) golden breadcrumbs
½ teaspoon hot chilli powder
3-4 pinches of cayenne pepper
vegetable oil for deep frying
sprigs of rosemary, sage and thyme, to garnish

Wrap and freeze portions of Camembert for 1 hour.

1 kg (2lb) pork spare ribs (sheets)
2 tablespoons dark soy sauce
1 tablespoon tomato purée (paste)
2 good pinches of Five-Spice Powder, see page 8
3 tablespoons clear honey
1 clove garlic, crushed
1 cm (½ in) piece fresh root ginger, peeled and grated
125 ml (4 fl oz/½ cup) unsweetened orange juice
¼ teaspoon prepared mustard
slices of orange peel, to garnish

Preheat oven to 190C (375F/Gas 5). Cut ribs into single portion ribs and arrange in a single layer in a large roasting dish.

On a plate, mix together the flour, mustard, herbs and season with pepper. Rub each portion of cheese thoroughly with the mixture, then dip into beaten egg. Mix breadcrumbs with chilli powder and cayenne pepper. Coat dipped cheese portions in mixture, pressing on firmly with palms of hands.

Mix the remaining ingredients together in a bowl until thoroughly combined. Spoon approximately half quantity over ribs and bake in oven for 30 minutes.

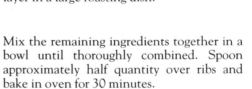

Half-fill a deep fat pan or fryer with oil and heat to 190C (375F) or until a cube of day-old bread browns in 40 seconds. Fry portions of cheese for about 30 seconds until golden brown. Drain on absorbent kitchen paper and serve at once, garnished with sprigs of rosemary, sage and thyme.

Serves 4.

Increase oven temperature to 200C (400F/Gas 6). Turn ribs and spoon over the remaining sauce. Bake for a further 50-60 minutes, basting and turning frequently until ribs are glazed and rich golden brown. Serve hot, garnished with slices of orange peel.

Serves 4.

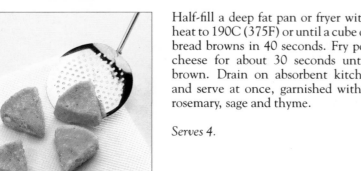

GUACAMOLE

2 ripe avocados
1 tablespoon lemon juice
1 small clove garlic, if desired
1 small fresh green chilli, seeded
1 shallot, finely chopped
1 tablespoon olive oil
few drops Tabasco sauce
salt
slices of lemon and sprig of parsley, to garnish
tortilla chips, to serve

Cut avocados in half, remove stones and scoop flesh onto a plate. Mash well.

Add lemon juice and garlic, if desired, and mix well. Very finely chop chilli and add to mixture together with chopped shallot.

Stir in oil, Tabasco sauce and salt and mix well together. Turn mixture into a serving bowl, garnish with slices of lemon and sprig of parsley and serve with tortilla chips.

Serves 4-6.

DEVILLED WHITEBAIT

375 g (12 oz) whitebait, thawed if frozen
30 g (1 oz/¼ cup) plain flour
¼ teaspoon salt
1 teaspoon dry mustard
¼ teaspoon cayenne pepper
½ teaspoon paprika
finely grated peel of 1 lemon
vegetable oil for frying
1-2 tablespoons chopped fresh parsley, lemon peel
    and sprigs of dill, to garnish
lemon wedges, to serve

Rinse whitebait under cold running water. Pat dry on absorbent kitchen paper.

Mix together the flour, salt, mustard, cayenne pepper, paprika and lemon peel in a polythene bag. Add whitebait and shake well until fish are evenly coated. Half-fill a deep fat pan or fryer with oil and heat to 190C (375F) or until a cube of day-old bread browns in 40 seconds. Place half whitebait in frying basket and lower gradually into hot oil and fry for 1 minute only, shaking basket frequently. Drain on absorbent kitchen paper.

Repeat with remaining whitebait. Reheat oil to same temperature. Place whole quantity whitebait into basket and fry for 1-2 minutes until lightly golden and crisp. Drain on absorbent kitchen paper. Turn into a warmed serving dish and garnish with chopped parsley, lemon peel and sprigs of dill. Serve hot with lemon wedges.

Serves 4.

SESAME PRAWN TOASTS

MULLIGATAWNY SOUP

185 g (6 oz) peeled prawns, thawed if frozen
2 cm (¾ in) piece fresh root ginger, peeled and grated
1 clove garlic, crushed
2 teaspoons cornflour
1 egg white
3 pinches of Five-Spice Powder, see page 8
salt and pepper
4 thin slices white bread, crusts removed
3 tablespoons sesame seeds
vegetable oil for shallow frying
spring onion flowers, to garnish

Drain prawns thoroughly on absorbent kitchen paper.

30 g (1 oz/6 teaspoons) butter
1 tablespoon corn oil
1 large onion, chopped
2 celery sticks, sliced thinly
3 carrots, diced
4 teaspoons Curry Powder, see page 8
6 teaspoons plain flour
1.2 litres (40 fl oz/5 cups) chicken stock
30 g (1 oz/2 tablespoons) long-grain rice
2 tomatoes, skinned and chopped
250 g (8 oz) cooked chicken, diced
1 small cooking apple, peeled, cored and diced
  salt
carrot twist and celery leaves, to garnish

Heat butter and oil in a saucepan.

Mince prawns finely and mix with ginger, garlic and cornflour. In a bowl, lightly whisk egg white with a fork (just enough to make frothy) and add to mixture. Stir in five-spice powder and seasoning and mix well together.

Add onion, celery and carrots and cook gently for 5 minutes. Stir in curry powder and flour and cook for 1 minute. Stir in stock and bring to the boil, then add rice and stir well.

Press prawn mixture evenly and firmly onto slices of bread. Sprinkle with sesame seeds and press on firmly. Heat 2 cm (¾ in) oil in a large frying pan. Lower slices, prawn-sides down, into hot oil and fry for 2-3 minutes until golden brown. Keep slices immersed in oil all the time, by pressing with a fish slice. Drain on absorbent kitchen paper. Cut into fingers and serve hot, garnished with spring onion flowers.

Serves 4.

Cover and simmer for 20 minutes, stirring occasionally. Add tomatoes, chicken and apple. Season with salt, then cover again and simmer for 15 minutes. Serve hot, garnished with a carrot twist and celery leaves.

Serves 4.

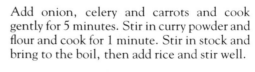

BEEF SATAY

3 tablespoons corn oil
1 small onion, finely chopped
1 clove garlic, crushed
½ teaspoon hot chilli powder
1-1½ teaspoons Curry Powder, see page 8
185 g (6 oz) crunchy peanut butter
1 teaspoon light soft brown sugar
2 teaspoons dark soy sauce
1 teaspoon lemon juice
salt and pepper
500 g (1 lb) rump steak
lemon slices and coriander leaves, to garnish

Heat 2 tablespoons oil in a saucepan. Add onion and garlic and fry gently until golden.

Add chilli powder, curry powder, 315 ml (10 fl oz/1¼ cups) water, peanut butter and sugar and bring to the boil. Simmer gently until thickened. Stir in soy sauce and lemon juice, then season with salt and pepper. Turn mixure into a serving dish.

Cut meat into 1 cm (½ in) cubes. Thread (not too tightly) onto 8 bamboo skewers, leaving a space at each end for holding. Cover ends with small pieces of foil. Place skewers in a greased grill pan. Brush with reserved 1 tablespoon oil. Cook under a hot grill for 10-15 minutes until golden and cooked through. Turn and brush frequently with oil during cooking. Serve hot, garnished with lemon slices and coriander leaves, with the peanut sauce.

Serves 4.

CURRY CREAM MUSSELS

1 kg (2 lb) mussels, cleaned, see page 12
155 ml (5 fl oz/¾ cup) dry cider
3 sprigs of thyme
1 clove garlic, crushed
30 g (1 oz/6 teaspoons) butter
3 shallots, finely chopped
1 stick celery, finely chopped
3 teaspoons Curry Powder, see page 8
3 teaspoons plain flour
60 ml (2 fl oz/¼ cup) single (light) cream
60 ml (2 fl oz/¼ cup) mayonnaise
sprigs of dill or parsley, to garnish
hot crusty bread, to serve

Place cleaned mussels in a large saucepan with 155 ml (5 fl oz/⅔ cup) water, cider, thyme and garlic. Cover and cook over high heat, shaking pan frequently, for 6-7 minutes, or until shells open. Discard any mussels which remain closed. Leave mussels to cool in liquor. Drain off cooled liquor, discarding thyme, then strain through a fine sieve and reserve. Remove a half shell from each mussel and arrange mussels on 4 serving plates.

Melt butter in a pan. Add shallots and celery and cook gently for 5 minutes. Add curry powder and flour and cook for 1 minute. Stir in 250 ml (8 fl oz/1 cup) reserved liquor and bring to the boil, stirring. Cover and cook gently for 10 minutes, stirring frequently. Cool. Stir in cream and mayonnaise and mix well. Spoon sauce over mussels and garnish with sprigs of dill or parsley. Serve with hot crusty bread.

Serves 4

GADO GADO

PEPPERED FARMHOUSE PÂTÉ

250 g (8 oz) white cabbage
60 ml (2 fl oz/¼ cup) sesame oil
1 large onion, quartered and thinly sliced
1 green pepper (capsicum), seeded and thinly sliced
185 g (6 oz) fresh beansprouts
1 fresh green chilli, seeded and finely chopped
1 clove garlic, crushed
2 shallots, finely chopped
½ teaspoon ground cumin
125 g (4 oz) smooth peanut butter
3 tablespoons lemon juice
few drops Tabasco sauce
red pepper (capsicum) strips, to garnish

Finely shred cabbage, discarding stalk.

Heat 2 tablespoons oil in a large frying pan. Add shredded cabbage, onion, green pepper (capsicum), beansprouts and chilli and fry over fairly high heat for 3-4 minutes, stirring all the time. Remove from heat, turn mixture into a serving dish and leave to cool.

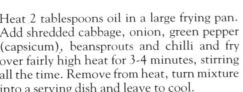

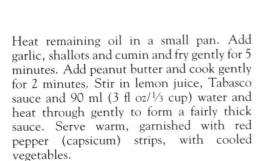

Heat remaining oil in a small pan. Add garlic, shallots and cumin and fry gently for 5 minutes. Add peanut butter and cook gently for 2 minutes. Stir in lemon juice, Tabasco sauce and 90 ml (3 fl oz/⅓ cup) water and heat through gently to form a fairly thick sauce. Serve warm, garnished with red pepper (capsicum) strips, with cooled vegetables.

Serves 4-6.

8 rashers smoked streaky bacon
500 g (1 lb) belly pork rashers
375 g (12 oz) pig's liver
1 onion, quartered
1 clove garlic
250 g (8 oz) veal escalope
1 egg, beaten
1 teaspoon salt
2 teaspoons green peppercorns
1 teaspoon dried mixed herbs
2 tablespoons brandy
green peppercorns and bay leaf, to garnish
crusty bread, to serve

Preheat oven to 180C (350F/Gas 4). Remove rinds and bones from bacon and pork.

Stretch bacon rashers on a board with the back of a knife until almost double in length. Use to line base and sides of a 1.2 litre (40 fl oz/5 cup) terrine or soufflé dish. Mince belly pork, liver, onion and garlic into a bowl. Cut veal into 1 cm (½ in) pieces and add to bowl. Stir in beaten egg, salt, peppercorns, herbs and brandy and mix thoroughly.

Spoon mixture into bacon-lined dish and smooth over surface. Cover tightly with foil. Put into a roasting tin, half-filled with hot water. Bake in oven for 2 hours. Cool for 30 minutes, then top with a plate and weight down with a heavy weight. Leave to cool completely, then refrigerate overnight. Turn out onto a serving plate. Serve, garnished with green peppercorns and a bay leaf, with crusty bread.

Serves 8.

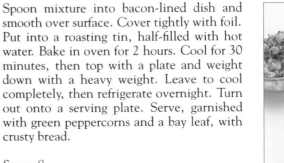

ORANGE GINGER DUCKLING

2 kg (4 lb) oven-ready duckling
250 g (8 oz) mange tout (snow peas)
1 red pepper (capsicum), seeded
3 tablespoons corn oil
3 sticks celery, sliced diagonally
12 spring onions, sliced diagonally
7.5 cm (3 in) piece fresh root ginger, peeled and chopped
1 tablespoon granulated sugar
1 tablespoon soy sauce
1 tablespoon dry sherry
1 tablespoon malt vinegar
1 tablespoon tomato purée (paste)
2 teaspoons cornflour
155 ml (5 fl oz/⅔ cup) orange juice
orange slices and mange tout (snow peas), to garnish

Preheat oven to 180C (350F/Gas 4). Prick duckling skin all over with a fork and put in a roasting tin. Bake in oven for 1¾ hours until golden and cooked. Top and tail mange tout (snow peas). Cut red pepper (capsicum) into small diamonds. Leave duck to cool, then strip flesh and skin from carcass. Cut into thin strips. Heat 2 tablespoons oil in a large frying pan. Add mange tout (snow peas) and celery and stir-fry for 2 minutes. Add spring onions, red pepper (capsicum) and ginger and stir-fry for 2 minutes. Remove from pan and keep warm.

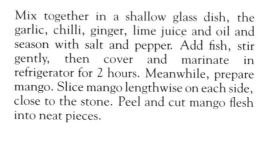

Heat remaining oil in pan. Add duckling and stir-fry 2 minutes. Remove from pan. Mix sugar, soy sauce, sherry, vinegar and tomato purée (paste) in a bowl. Blend cornflour with a little orange juice. Add rest of juice. Add to bowl. Stir into pan. Bring to boil, stirring. Lower heat and simmer 2 minutes. Return vegetables and duckling to pan; heat. Serve, garnished with orange and mange tout.

Serves 4.

Note: Serve with rice and prawn crackers.

TROPICAL FISH KEBABS

1 kg (2 lb) monkfish
2 cloves garlic, crushed
1 fresh green chilli, seeded and chopped
2.5 cm (1 in) piece fresh root ginger, peeled and chopped
juice of 1 lime
75 ml (2½ fl oz/⅓ cup) corn oil
salt and pepper
1 ripe mango
2 bananas
1 red pepper (capsicum), seeded and cubed
rice salad, to serve
wedges of lime, to garnish

Cut away monkfish from central bone. Cut flesh into neat bite-sized pieces.

Mix together in a shallow glass dish, the garlic, chilli, ginger, lime juice and oil and season with salt and pepper. Add fish, stir gently, then cover and marinate in refrigerator for 2 hours. Meanwhile, prepare mango. Slice mango lengthwise on each side, close to the stone. Peel and cut mango flesh into neat pieces.

Cut bananas into chunky pieces. Thread pieces of fish onto 4 long (or 8 short) bamboo skewers, alternating fish with cubes of red pepper (capsicum), mango and banana. Arrange skewers in a grill pan and spoon over marinade. Cook under grill for 12-15 minutes, turning frequently and spooning with marinade, until cooked through. Serve hot with rice salad, garnished with wedges of lime.

Serves 4.

SINGAPORE PARCELS

125 g (4 oz/1 cup) plain flour
1 large egg
155 ml (5 fl oz/⅔ cup) milk
5 tablespoons corn oil
250 g (8 oz) lean minced beef
1 onion, chopped
2 carrots, grated
1 parsnip, grated
2 teaspoons Curry Powder, see page 8
3 teaspoons tomato purée (paste)
2 teaspoons cornflour
155 ml (5 fl oz/⅔ cup) beef stock
a little beaten egg for brushing
vegetable oil for deep frying
carrot strips, to garnish

Heat 3 tablespoons oil in a saucepan. Add minced beef, onion, carrots, parsnip and curry powder and cook gently for 5 minutes, stirring. Add tomato purée (paste) and mix well. Blend cornflour with a little stock. Add remaining stock to pan and bring to the boil. Add cornflour mixture and cook for 2 minutes, stirring all the time. Simmer mixture for 10 minutes. Leave until cold.

Sift flour into a bowl. Make a well in centre and add egg. Gradually stir in milk and beat well until smooth. Stir in 155 ml (5 fl oz/⅔ cup) cold water and beat well. Pour batter into a jug.

Put pancakes, cooked-sides up, on a work surface and spread filling in a 5 cm (2 in) horizontal line across centre to within 4 cm (1½ in) of side edges. Fold these side edges over mixture and then fold the remaining top and bottom edges over to cover filling. Brush with beaten egg. Chill for 1 hour.

Heat a little oil in a 15-17.5 cm (6-7 in) frying pan and pour off excess. Pour a little batter into pan, swirling pan to spread batter evenly over base to make a thin coating. Cook until underside is golden, then turn pancake out of pan (do not cook other side). Cook remaining batter in the same way, adding more oil to pan each time, to make 8 pancakes.

Half-fill a deep fat pan or fryer with oil and heat to 190C (375F) or until a cube of day-old bread browns in 40 seconds. Fry parcels, 4 at a time, for 2-3 minutes until golden brown and heated through. Drain on absorbent kitchen paper and serve hot, garnished with carrot strips.

Serves 8.

DEVILLED CRAB QUICHE

250 g (8 oz/2 cups) plain flour
½ teaspoon salt
½ teaspoon chilli seasoning
60 g (2 oz/¼ cup) block margarine, diced
60 g (2 oz/¼ cup) lard, diced
60 g (2 oz/½ cup) finely grated Cheddar cheese
6 rashers streaky bacon, chopped
1 onion, chopped
125 g (4 oz) crabmeat, flaked
3 eggs
155 ml (5 fl oz/⅔ cup) single (light) cream
½ teaspoon dry mustard
¼ teaspoon cayenne pepper
tomato and sprig of parsley, to garnish

Preheat oven to 200C (400F/Gas 6).

Put flour, salt and chilli seasoning into a bowl. Add margarine and lard and rub in finely until mixture resembles breadcrumbs. Add cheese and mix well. Stir in 3 tablespoons water and mix to form a firm dough. Knead gently. Roll out pastry and use to line a 25 cm (10 in) loose-bottomed, fluted flan tin, set on a baking sheet. Press pastry well into flutes and trim edge neatly. Prick base all over with a fork. Line flan with a piece of greaseproof paper and fill with baking beans.

Bake in the oven for 15 minutes, then remove paper and beans and return flan to oven for a further 5-10 minutes until dry and lightly golden. Meanwhile, dry-fry bacon in a pan for 3 minutes. Add onion and cook for 2 minutes. Remove from heat and mix with crabmeat. Spoon mixture into flan case. Whisk together eggs, cream, mustard and cayenne and season with salt. Pour into flan case. Bake for 30-35 minutes until golden. Serve, garnished with tomato and parsley.

Serves 6-8.

MUSTARD PORK

15 g (½ oz/3 teaspoons) butter
1 tablespoon vegetable oil
4 pork steaks, each weighing about 185 g (6 oz)
1 onion, finely chopped
1 clove garlic, crushed
1 tablespoon wholegrain or Dijon mustard
4 tablespoons dry white wine
3 tablespoons single (light) cream
salt and pepper
155 g (5 oz) Mozzarella cheese, chopped
lemon wedges, to garnish
celery, cucumber and watercress, to serve

Heat butter and oil in a frying pan. Add pork steaks and fry for 3 minutes on each side.

Cover and cook gently for 15 minutes, turning occasionally. Remove pork steaks from pan and keep warm in a shallow flameproof dish. Add onion and garlic to pan and cook for 5 minutes.

Add mustard and wine to pan, stir well, then bring to the boil and boil for 1½ minutes. Stir in cream and heat through gently, then season with salt and pepper. Spoon mixture over pork steaks and sprinkle with chopped Mozzarella cheese. Cook under grill for 5 minutes until cheese is melted and bubbling. Serve hot, garnished with lemon wedges, with a salad of celery, cucumber and watercress.

Serves 4.

CHILLI BEAN TACOS

TANGY DRUMSTICKS

2 tablespoons olive oil
500 g (1 lb) pork sausagemeat, crumbled
1 onion, chopped
1 clove garlic, crushed
½ teaspoon ground cumin
1 teaspoon hot chilli powder
1 tomato, skinned and chopped
3 tablespoons tomato purée (paste)
½ a red pepper (capsicum), seeded and diced
315 g (10 oz) can kidney beans, drained
salt
8 taco shells
thick sour cream, paprika, lettuce leaves and radish
    roses, to serve

1 small onion, chopped
1 tablespoon clear honey
1 clove garlic, crushed
3 tablespoons corn oil
3 tablespoons tomato ketchup (sauce)
1 tablespoon tomato purée (paste)
2 teaspoons Worcestershire sauce
1 teaspoon chilli sauce
2 pinches of Five-Spice Powder, see page 8
8 chicken drumsticks
cress and slices of lemon, to garnish

In a small saucepan, mix together onion,
honey, garlic, 2 tablespoons oil, tomato
ketchup (sauce) and purée (paste).

Preheat oven to 180C (350F/Gas 4). Heat oil
in a saucepan. Add sausagemeat, onion,
garlic, cumin and chilli powder and fry gently
for 5 minutes, stirring to break up
sausagemeat. Add tomato, tomato purée
(paste), red pepper (capsicum) and kidney
beans. Stir well and cook gently for 15
minutes, stirring frequently to prevent
mixture sticking. Season with salt.

Add Worcestershire sauce, chilli sauce and
five-spice powder and simmer, uncovered, for
5 minutes, stirring occasionally. Blend
mixture to a smooth purée in a blender or
food processor. Add remaining oil and stir
well.

Meanwhile, heat taco shells in the oven,
following packet instructions. Fill hot taco
shells with sausagemeat mixture. Top each
one with a spoonful of thick sour cream and
sprinkle with paprika. Serve with lettuce
leaves and radish roses.

Serves 4-8.

Arrange chicken drumsticks in a roasting tin.
Brush with marinade and leave to marinate
for 1 hour. Preheat oven to 200C (400F/Gas
6). Bake in oven for 35-40 minutes, turning
and brushing frequently with marinade
juices. Serve hot or cold, garnished with
cress and lemon slices.

Serves 4.

CLAM & PRAWN CHOWDER

PORK & PEPPERS

60 g (2 oz/¼ cup) butter
1 large onion, chopped
2 sticks celery, chopped
2 potatoes, diced
1½ teaspoon fennel seeds
6 teaspoons plain flour
1 teaspoon paprika
470 ml (15 fl oz/1¾ cups) chicken stock
315 g (10 oz) can baby clams, drained
125 g (4 oz) peeled prawns, thawed if frozen
1 red pepper (capsicum), seeded and diced
125 g (4 oz) frozen sweetcorn, thawed
155 ml (5 fl oz/⅔ cup) single (light) cream
salt and pepper
sprigs of dill, to garnish

3 pinches of Five-Spice powder, see page 8
2 tablespoons dry sherry or sake
2 tablespoons light soy sauce
1 clove garlic, crushed
2.5 cm (1 in) piece fresh root ginger, peeled and
    chopped
500 g (1 lb) pork tenderloin, cut into thin strips
2 onions
1 red pepper (capsicum), seeded
1 green pepper (capsicum), seeded
4 tablespoons corn oil
90 g (3 oz) button mushrooms, sliced
6 canned whole water chestnuts, sliced
2 teaspoons cornflour
155 ml (5 fl oz/⅔ cup) chicken stock
leek and spring onion curls, to garnish

Melt butter in a saucepan. Add onion, celery, potatoes and fennel seeds and cook gently for 5 minutes, stirring frequently. Blend in flour and cook for 1 minute. Stir in paprika and stock and bring to the boil, stirring.

In a bowl, mix together five-spice powder, sherry or sake, soy sauce, garlic and ginger. Add pork, stir well and marinate for 30 minutes. Cut onions into eighths and separate into layers. Cut peppers (capsicums) into thin strips. Heat 2 tablespoons oil in a large frying pan or wok. Drain pork from marinade (reserving marinade), add to pan and stir-fry for 5 minutes. Remove from pan and keep warm.

Reduce heat and simmer, covered, for 15 minutes, stirring occasionally. Add clams, prawns, red pepper (capsicum) and sweetcorn and simmer for a further 5 minutes. Stir in cream and season with salt and pepper. Serve hot, garnished with dill.

Serves 4.

Variation: Omit paprika and add 1 teaspoon Curry Powder, see page 8. Add 1 tablespoon chopped fresh parsley or coriander just before serving.

Add remaining oil to pan. Add onions, peppers (capsicums), mushrooms and water chestnuts and stir-fry for 3 minutes. Add mixture to pork. Blend cornflour with reserved marinade and 2 tablespoons stock. Add remaining stock to pan and bring to the boil. Add cornflour mixture and cook for 2 minutes, stirring all the time. Return pork and vegetables to pan and heat through, stirring all the time. Serve hot, garnished with leek and spring onion curls.

Serves 4.

STEAK AU POIVRE

1½ teaspoons green peppercorns
1 teaspoon black peppercorns
1 teaspoon white peppercorns
4 rump steaks, each weighing about 185 g (6 oz)
45 g (1½ oz/9 teaspoons) unsalted butter
few drops Tabasco sauce
few drops Worcestershire sauce
2 tablespoons brandy
3 tablespoons double (thick) cream
salt
sauté or jacket baked potatoes and green salad, to serve

Coarsely crush all peppercorns in a pestle and mortar.

Sprinkle crushed pepper over both sides of steaks, pressing in well with palm of hand. Set aside for 30 minutes. Melt 15 g (½ oz/3 teaspoons) butter in a large frying pan and heat until foaming. Add steaks and cook for 2-3 minutes, then turn and cook other sides for 2-3 minutes. (This timing gives medium-rare steaks, so adjust cooking time to suit personal preference). Turn steaks once again and top each one with 7 g (¼ oz/1½ teaspoons) butter and sprinkle with a few drops Tabasco sauce and Worcestershire sauce.

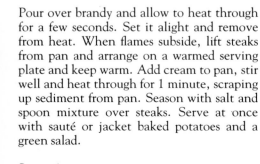

Pour over brandy and allow to heat through for a few seconds. Set it alight and remove from heat. When flames subside, lift steaks from pan and arrange on a warmed serving plate and keep warm. Add cream to pan, stir well and heat through for 1 minute, scraping up sediment from pan. Season with salt and spoon mixture over steaks. Serve at once with sauté or jacket baked potatoes and a green salad.

Serves 4.

CREOLE JAMBALAYA

2 tablespoons olive oil
250 g (8 oz) piece ham, diced
250 g (8 oz) chorizo sausage, sliced
1 large Spanish onion, chopped
3 cloves garlic, crushed
½ teaspoon dried thyme
2 tablespoons chopped fresh parsley
375 ml (12 fl oz/1½ cups) boiling chicken stock
315 g (10 oz) long-grain rice
¼ teaspoon cayenne pepper
1 teaspoon Tabasco sauce
440 g (14 oz) can tomatoes
1 green pepper (capsicum), seeded and diced
2 tablespoons dry white wine
tomato and sprigs of thyme, to garnish

Heat oil in a saucepan. Add ham, chorizo sausage and onion and fry gently for 3 minutes. Add garlic, thyme and parsley and stir well, then add stock, rice, cayenne and Tabasco sauce and mix well. Add tomatoes and break up with a spoon. Bring mixture to the boil, stir well, then cover and simmer gently for 15 minutes.

Add green pepper (capsicum) and wine, stir well, then cover and continue cooking for a further 8 minutes or until liquid is absorbed. Fluff up with a fork and serve hot, garnished with tomato and thyme.

Serves 4-6.

Variations: Add 125 g (4 oz) peeled prawns (thawed, if frozen) to mixture 5 minutes before the end of cooking time.

For a more fiery flavour, increase cayenne and Tabasco sauce, according to taste.

VEGETABLE COUSCOUS

250 g (8 oz) couscous
4 tablespoons olive oil
2 onions, coarsely chopped
1 large aubergine (eggplant), diced
500 g (1 lb) acorn squash, seeded and diced
2 carrots, sliced
1 teaspoon Harissa, see page 8
2 tomatoes, skinned and chopped
2 tablespoons tomato purée (paste)
470 ml (15 fl oz/2 cups) vegetable stock
410 g (13 oz) can chick peas, drained
2 courgettes (zucchini), sliced
60 g (2 oz/⅓ cup) sultanas or raisins
2 tablespoons chopped fresh parsley
sprig of coriander or parsley, to garnish

Put couscous in a bowl with 470 ml (15 fl oz/2 cups) water. Leave to soak for 15 minutes until water is absorbed. Heat oil in a saucepan. Add onions, aubergine (egg plant), squash and carrots and fry for 5 minutes, stirring frequently. Stir in harissa, tomatoes, tomato purée (paste) and stock. Bring to the boil and stir well. Line a large metal sieve or colander with muslin or all purpose kitchen cloth and place over pan.

Put couscous into sieve. Cover whole pan with foil to enclose steam, then simmer for 20 minutes. Add chick peas, courgettes (zucchini) and sultanas or raisins to pan, stir well, then replace sieve and fluff up couscous with a fork. Cover again with foil and simmer for a further 20 minutes. Spread couscous on a large serving dish and fluff up with a fork. Add parsley to mixture in pan and spoon mixture over couscous. Serve hot, garnished with sprig of coriander or parsley.

Serves 4-6.

CHEESE CHILLI BURGERS

2 tablespoons olive oil
2 onions, finely chopped
2 cloves garlic, crushed
250 g (8 oz) can tomatoes
100 g (3½ oz) can green chillies in brine
1 tablespoon chilli relish
½ teaspoon cumin seeds
500 g (1 lb) lean ground beef
salt and pepper
2 tablespoons corn oil
4 slices Gruyére cheese
shredded lettuce
4 warmed baps, split
raw onion rings

In a saucepan, heat olive oil. Add 1 chopped onion and garlic cloves and fry gently for 5 minutes. Purée tomatoes in a blender or food processor. Drain and chop chillies. Add tomatoes, chillies, chilli relish and cumin seeds to pan. Stir well, then cover and simmer for 10 minutes, stirring occasionally.

Put beef into a bowl. Add remaining onion and salt and pepper. Mix well together. Divide into 4 portions and shape each into a 10.5 cm (4½ in) round burger. Heat corn oil in a large frying pan. Add burgers and fry for 5-6 minutes on each side. Top each with a slice of cheese. Arrange lettuce on base of each bap. Place a burger on each and top with chilli sauce and onion rings. Cover with lids and serve hot.

Serves 4.

CHILLI CON CARNE

NASI GORENG

2 tablespoons olive oil
625 g (1¼ lb) lean minced beef
2 onions, chopped
1 clove garlic, crushed
2 sticks celery, chopped
2 teaspoons hot chilli powder
1 teaspoon cumin seeds
440 g (14 oz) can tomatoes
2 tablespoons tomato purée (paste)
470 g (15 oz) can red kidney beans, drained
1 teaspoon salt
boiled rice, thick sour cream, diced avocado and raw
    onion rings, to serve

Preheat oven to 180C (350F/Gas 4). Heat oil in flameproof casserole.

250 g (8 oz/1½ cups) long-grain rice
3 tablespoons corn oil
2 onions, halved and sliced
2 cloves garlic, crushed
2 small fresh green chillies, seeded and chopped
185 g (6 oz) pork tenderloin, diced
185 g (6 oz) skinned chicken breast (fillets), diced
¼ teaspoon hot chilli powder
1 teaspoon paprika
2 tablespoons light soy sauce
125 g (4 oz) peeled prawns, thawed if frozen
salt
1 egg
7 g (¼ oz/1½ teaspoons) butter
prawn crackers, to serve

Add minced beef, onions, garlic and celery and fry gently for 5 minutes, stirring occasionally. Add chilli powder and cumin and cook gently for 2 minutes. Add tomatoes, and break up with a spoon. Stir in tomato purée (paste) and kidney beans. Bring to the boil, stirring.

Cook rice in boiling, salted water for 12 minutes. Drain and rinse well, then drain again. Heat oil in a large frying pan. Add onions, garlic and chillies and fry for 2 minutes. Add pork and chicken and fry gently for 10 minutes until cooked. Add chilli powder, paprika, soy sauce, prawns and rice and cook for 5-6 minutes until piping hot, stirring all the time. Season with salt.

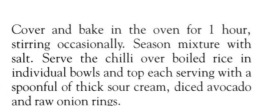

Cover and bake in the oven for 1 hour, stirring occasionally. Season mixture with salt. Serve the chilli over boiled rice in individual bowls and top each serving with a spoonful of thick sour cream, diced avocado and raw onion rings.

Serves 4.

Note: To prevent avocado discolouring, toss in lemon juice.

For a more fiery flavour, add 3 teaspoons chilli powder at step 2.

Turn mixture into a warm serving dish and keep warm, while preparing omelette topping. Whisk egg with 1 teaspoon water. Melt butter in a frying pan. Add egg mixture and swirl pan to give a thin, even mixture. Cook over gentle heat for 2-3 minutes until set and lightly golden underneath. Turn omelette out onto a board. Roll up and cut into slices. Arrange slices of omelette on top of rice mixture. Serve hot with prawn crackers.

Serves 4.

INDONESIAN BEEF

750 g (1½ lb) topside of beef, cut into slices
3 tablespoons corn oil
1 large Spanish onion, sliced
1 clove garlic, crushed
1 teaspoon ground ginger
1 teaspoon ground cumin
1 teaspoon ground coriander
1 teaspoon chilli seasoning
60 g (2 oz/⅔ cup) desiccated coconut
2 teaspoons light soft brown sugar
1 tablespoon lemon juice
315 ml (10 fl oz/1¼ cups) beef stock
thin slivers of red pepper (capsicum) and green chilli
   and small onion rings, to garnish

CHILLI PEPPER PIZZA

3 tablespoons olive oil
1 onion, quartered and sliced
1 clove garlic, crushed
250 g (8 oz) can tomatoes
1 tablespoon tomato purée (paste)
½ teaspoon dried oregano
125 g (4 oz/1 cup) plain flour
125 g (4 oz/1 cup) plain wholewheat flour
¼ teaspoon salt
1 teaspoon easy blend dried yeast
155 ml (5 fl oz/⅔ cup) hand-hot water
100 g (3½ oz) can green chillies in brine
185 g (6 oz) Mozzarella cheese, chopped
60 g (2 oz) pepperoni salami sticks, sliced
8 black or green olives
tomato roses and sprigs of parsley, to garnish

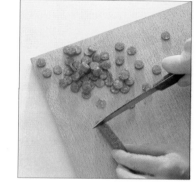

Cut slices of topside into 1 cm (½ in) thick strips. Heat oil in a saucepan. Add onion and garlic and fry gently until soft. Add meat and fry, stirring, until browned all over.

Heat 2 tablespoons oil in a saucepan. Add onion, garlic, tomatoes, tomato purée (paste) and oregano. Stir well to break up tomatoes, then simmer, uncovered, for 10-15 minutes until well thickened. Leave to cool. Preheat oven to 190C (375F/Gas 5). Put flours, salt and yeast into a bowl and mix well. Add water and mix to form a dough. Knead well, then roll out to a round large enough to line a lightly greased 25 cm (10 in) pizza tray.

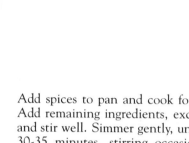

Add spices to pan and cook for 2 minutes. Add remaining ingredients, except garnish, and stir well. Simmer gently, uncovered, for 30-35 minutes, stirring occasionally, until mixture is thickened and dry. Stir mixture more frequently towards the end of cooking time to prevent it sticking. Serve hot, garnished liberally with thin slivers of red pepper (capsicum) and green chilli and small onion rings.

Serves 4.

Brush surface of dough with a little of the remaining oil and cover with tomato mixture. Drain and chop chillies and sprinkle on top. Scatter with chopped cheese and drizzle with remaining oil. Bake in the oven for 25 minutes. Add sliced pepperoni and olives to pizza and continue cooking for a further 10 minutes. Serve hot, cut into wedges, garnished with tomato roses and sprigs of parsley.

Serves 2 (as a meal) or 4 (as a snack).

VEGETARIAN MEDLEY

SPANISH OMELETTE

125 g (4 oz/¾ cup) whole green lentils
125 g (4 oz/¾ cup) split peas
2 leeks, cut into 0.5 cm (¼ in) slices
2 courgettes (zucchini), cut into 0.5 cm (¼ in) slices
2 carrots, thinly sliced
2 sticks celery, thinly sliced
1 onion, coarsely chopped
1 clove garlic, crushed
30 g (1 oz/6 teaspoons) ghee
½ teaspoon turmeric
1 teaspoon mustard seeds
2 teaspoons Garam Masala, see page 8
salt
celery leaves and slices of lemon, to garnish

1 tablespoon olive oil
15 g (½ oz/3 teaspoons) butter
1 onion, chopped
1 clove garlic, crushed
1 red pepper (capsicum), seeded and diced
90 g (3 oz) green cabbage, finely shredded
4 rashers streaky bacon, chopped
1 teaspoon fenugreek
½ teaspoon ground coriander
4 eggs, beaten
salt and pepper
60 g (2 oz/½ cup) grated Cheddar cheese
strips of red pepper (capsicum) and sprigs of parsley, to garnish
salad and crusty bread, to serve

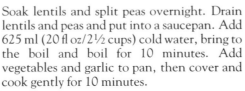

Soak lentils and split peas overnight. Drain lentils and peas and put into a saucepan. Add 625 ml (20 fl oz/2½ cups) cold water, bring to the boil and boil for 10 minutes. Add vegetables and garlic to pan, then cover and cook gently for 10 minutes.

Heat oil and butter in a 17.5-20 cm (7-8 in) frying pan. Add onion, garlic, red pepper (capsicum), cabbage and bacon and fry over gentle heat for 5 minutes, stirring occasionally. Add fenugreek and coriander and stir well.

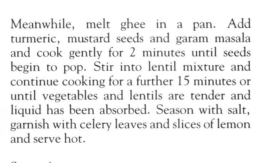

Meanwhile, melt ghee in a pan. Add turmeric, mustard seeds and garam masala and cook gently for 2 minutes until seeds begin to pop. Stir into lentil mixture and continue cooking for a further 15 minutes or until vegetables and lentils are tender and liquid has been absorbed. Season with salt, garnish with celery leaves and slices of lemon and serve hot.

Serves 4.

Whisk eggs with 1 tablespoon cold water and salt and pepper, then pour into pan. Swirl pan to ensure an even coating. Cook over gentle heat for 3-4 minutes until mixture is golden brown underneath. Sprinkle surface with grated cheese and place pan under a preheated grill and cook until mixture is set on top and cheese has melted. Cut into 4 portions and serve hot, garnished with strips of red pepper (capsicum) and sprigs of parsley, with salad and crusty bread.

Serves 4.

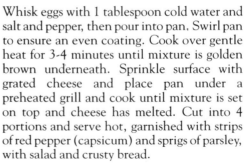

FALAFEL

CEYLONESE CURRY

410 g (13 oz) can chick peas, drained
1 onion, quartered
2 cloves garlic
125 g (4 oz) fresh white bread
¼ teaspoon cumin seeds
4 small dried red chillies, crushed
1 tablespoon chopped fresh parsley
salt and pepper
1 egg, beaten
45 g (1½ oz/⅓ cup) golden breadcrumbs
vegetable oil for deep frying
4 warmed pitta bread, shredded lettuce, sliced onion
   and sliced tomato, to serve

2 large onions
5 cm (2 in) piece fresh root ginger
2 cloves garlic
5 tablespoons corn oil
2½-3 tablespoons Curry Powder, see page 8
750 g (1½ lb) boneless chicken breasts, skinned
4 teaspoons plain flour
375 ml (12 fl oz/1½ cups) chicken stock
1 red or green pepper (capsicum), seeded
2 sticks celery, sliced
½ teaspoon cumin seeds
90 g (3 oz) button mushrooms, if desired
22 g (¾ oz) creamed coconut, chopped
2 large tomatoes, peeled, seeded and sliced
toasted shredded coconut and chervil sprigs, to garnish

Put chick peas, onion, garlic, bread, cumin seeds and chillies in a blender or food processor. Process ingredients until smooth, then turn mixture into a bowl. Add parsley, salt and pepper and beaten egg and mix well. Form into 8 balls and coat in breadcrumbs. Flatten each one slightly to form oval shapes.

Put one of the onions into a blender or food processor. Chop ginger and add with garlic and 2 tablespoons water. Blend until very finely chopped. Heat 3 tablespoons oil in a saucepan. Add onion and ginger mixture and curry powder and fry for 2 minutes, stirring all the time. Cut chicken into bite-sized cubes and add to pan. Fry until sealed all over. Stir in flour and cook for 1 minute, then stir in stock and bring to the boil. Cover and simmer gently for 15 minutes.

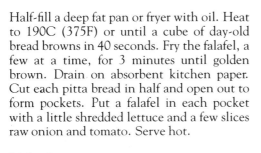

Half-fill a deep fat pan or fryer with oil. Heat to 190C (375F) or until a cube of day-old bread browns in 40 seconds. Fry the falafel, a few at a time, for 3 minutes until golden brown. Drain on absorbent kitchen paper. Cut each pitta bread in half and open out to form pockets. Put a falafel in each pocket with a little shredded lettuce and a few slices raw onion and tomato. Serve hot.

Makes 8.

Meanwhile, peel and slice remaining onion and separate into rings. Dice pepper (capsicum). Heat remaining oil in a frying pan. Add celery, onion rings, red pepper (capsicum), cumin seeds and mushrooms, if desired, and fry gently for 4 minutes. Add mixture to saucepan and continue cooking for a further 15 minutes. Stir in creamed coconut, then add tomato slices and heat through. Serve hot, garnished with shredded coconut and chervil.

Serves 4.

BARBECUE SAUCE

WINE & PEPPER SAUCE

3 tablespoons corn oil
1 small onion
1 clove garlic, crushed
½ teaspoon dry mustard
2 tablespoons malt vinegar
1 tablespoon Worcestershire sauce
2 tablespoons light soft brown sugar
3 tablespoons tomato ketchup (sauce)
½ teaspoon chilli seasoning
185 ml (6 fl oz/¾ cup) chicken stock
sprig of parsley, to garnish

30 g (1 oz/6 teaspoons) unsalted butter
2 shallots, finely chopped
1 tablespoon brandy
125 ml (4 fl oz/½ cup) dry white wine
125 ml (4 fl oz/½ cup) chicken stock
2 teaspoons green peppercorns, coarsely crushed
3 tablespoons double (thick) cream
1 tablespoon chopped fresh parsley
sprig of parsley, to garnish

Heat oil in a small saucepan. Add onion and garlic and cook gently for 2 minutes, stirring frequently.

Melt butter in a frying pan. Add shallots and cook gently for 3 minutes. Add brandy to pan and allow to heat through for a few seconds, then set it alight and when flames subside, add wine to pan.

Stir in mustard, vinegar, Worcestershire sauce, sugar, tomato ketchup (sauce), chilli seasoning and chicken stock. Bring to the boil.

Stir in stock and peppercorns and boil rapidly for 2-3 minutes until quantity is slightly reduced.

Cover and simmer sauce gently for 7-8 minutes until slightly thickened. Serve hot as a sauce, garnished with sprigs of parsley, with beefburgers, hot dogs or fried chicken. Or, if preferred, allow to cool and use to brush over meats, poultry and fish while baking or grilling.

Makes 315 ml (10 fl oz/1¼ cups).

Remove from heat and stir in cream and parsley. Return to medium heat and heat through for 2-3 minutes, stirring all the time. Serve hot, garnished with a sprig of parsley, with steaks, veal or fish dishes.

Makes 185 ml (6 fl oz/¾ cup).

TANGY MUSTARD SAUCE

45 g (1½ oz/9 teaspoons) butter
1 small onion, finely chopped
30 g (1 oz/¼ cup) plain flour
280 ml (9 fl oz/1 cup) chicken stock
155 ml (5 fl oz/⅔ cup) milk
1 bay leaf
1 teaspoon wholegrain mustard
2 teaspoons dry mustard
1 tablespoon wine vinegar
1 teaspoon caster sugar
salt and pepper
bay leaves, to garnish

Melt butter in a saucepan. Add onion and cook gently for 2 minutes. Stir in flour.

Cook for 1 minute. Stir in stock and bring to the boil, stirring. Reduce heat and simmer for 2 minutes, stirring all the time. Add milk and bay leaf, stir well and cook for 2 minutes.

Blend mustards smoothly with vinegar and sugar. Add mixture to pan and season with salt and pepper, then heat through for 2-3 minutes. Remove bay leaf. Serve sauce hot, garnished with bay leaves, with smoked sausage, rabbit or fish dishes.

Makes 470 ml (15 fl oz/1¾ cups).

Note: This recipe gives a good coating sauce, so if a pouring sauce is desired, simply add a little more stock or milk.

SPICY CHILLI SAUCE

1 clove garlic
1 Spanish onion, quartered
2 fresh green chillies, seeded
2 tablespoons corn oil
½ teaspoon ground ginger
250 g (8 oz) can tomatoes
60 g (2 oz/⅓ cup) seedless raisins
1 tablespoon lemon juice
1 tablespoon dark soy sauce
30 g (1 oz/2 tablespoons) light soft brown sugar
salt and pepper
sprig of parsley, to garnish

In a blender or food processor, finely chop garlic, onion and chillies.

Heat oil in a saucepan. Add onion mixture and ginger and cook gently for 3 minutes. Add tomatoes and break up with a spoon. Stir in raisins, lemon juice, soy sauce, sugar and 315 ml (10 fl oz/1¼ cups) water.

Bring to the boil, then reduce heat and simmer, uncovered, for 15 minutes. Blend to a smooth purée in a blender or food processor. Reheat and season with salt and pepper. Serve hot, garnished with a sprig of parsley, with grilled steak or fried chicken.

Makes 625 ml (20 fl oz/2½ cups).

Note: This sauce is also delicious served with grilled white fish.

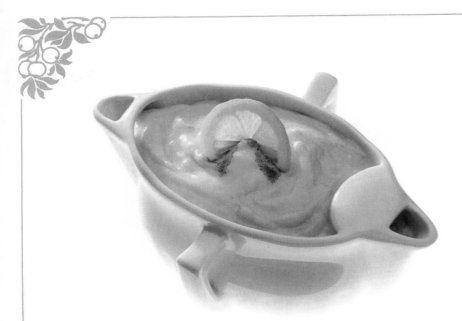

LEMON HOLLANDAISE

COCONUT SAUCE

60 ml (2 fl oz/¼ cup) lemon juice
1 teaspoon black peppercorns
3 blades of mace
2 large egg yolks
125 g (4 oz/½ cup) butter, at room temperature
3 good pinches of cayenne pepper
thin slice of lemon and paprika, to garnish

Put lemon juice, peppercorns and mace into a small saucepan. Bring to the boil and boil until liquid is reduced by half. Put egg yolks into a bowl with 15 g (½ oz/3 teaspoons) butter and beat well together.

Strain the hot lemon liquid onto butter mixture, beating well all the time with a wooden spoon. Return to pan and place over a very low heat. Gradually add small pieces of remaining butter, whisking really well all the time, until sauce is thickened and smooth. (If mixture gets too hot at this stage it will curdle and separate. To prevent this happening, keep removing pan from heat whilst beating in butter to ensure gentle cooking.)

Add cayenne pepper to sauce and mix well. Turn mixture into a warm serving dish. Garnish with a thin slice of lemon and a sprinkling of paprika. Serve warm or cold with poached salmon, asparagus or globe artichokes.

Makes 155 ml (5 fl oz/⅔ cup).

Note: Remember that this rich egg and butter-based sauce requires great care during cooking to achieve the delicious result.

90 g (3 oz/1 cup) desiccated coconut
410 ml (13 fl oz/1⅔ cups) boiling water
3 tablespoons corn oil
1 onion, quartered and thinly sliced
1 clove garlic, crushed
3 teaspoons Curry Powder, see page 8
½ teaspoon turmeric
½ teaspoon ground coriander
½ teaspoon hot chilli powder
3 teaspoons cornflour
1 tablespoon lemon juice
1 large tomato, skinned and seeded
½ small green pepper (capsicum), seeded
salt

Put coconut and boiling water into a blender or food processor and blend for 45 seconds. Pass mixture through a fine sieve, pressing coconut firmly to extract liquor. Heat oil in a saucepan. Add onion, garlic, curry powder, turmeric, coriander and chilli powder and fry gently for 3 minutes, stirring.

Add coconut milk and bring to the boil. Cover and simmer gently for 5 minutes. Blend cornflour with lemon juice and add to pan. Bring to the boil and cook for 2 minutes, stirring all the time. Cut tomato and green pepper (capsicum) into thin slivers and add to sauce. Cook gently for 5 minutes. Season with salt. Serve hot with grilled steak, chicken or stir-fry dishes.

Makes 560 ml (18 fl oz/2¼ cups).

ROAST PEPPER RELISH

1 yellow, 1 red and 1 green pepper (capsicum), halved and seeded
1 onion, quartered and thinly sliced
90 ml (3 fl oz/⅓ cup) corn oil
2 tablespoons lemon juice
1 teaspoon wholegrain mustard
1 clove garlic, crushed
½ teaspoon Garam Masala, see page 8
1½ teaspoons caster sugar
salt and pepper
sprigs of coriander, to garnish

Preheat oven to 200C (400F/Gas 6). Put peppers (capsicums) in a roasting tin.

Bake in the oven for 30 minutes or until skins begin to blister and blacken. Cool peppers (capsicums), then peel away thin skins. Cut peppers (capsicums) into quarters and slice into thin strips. Put peppers (capsicums) into a shallow dish. Sprinkle with onion.

Put remaining ingredients into a screw-top jar and shake vigorously until well blended. Pour mixture over peppers (capsicums) and marinate for several hours, stirring occasionally. Serve chilled, garnished with sprigs of coriander, as an accompaniment to game pies, cold meats or crusty bread and cheese.

Serves 4.

Note: This colourful relish keeps well in the refrigerator for up to 3 days.

PIQUANT ORIENTAL SAUCE

2 tablespoons corn oil
1 onion, quartered and thinly sliced
1 carrot, cut into fine matchstick strips
½ green pepper (capsicum), seeded and cut into thin strips
4 cm (1½ in) piece fresh root ginger, peeled and chopped
3 pinches of Five-Spice Powder, see page 8
250 g (8 oz) can pineapple slices
1 tablespoon granulated sugar
1 tablespoon dark soy sauce
1 tablespoon dry sherry
1 tablespoon malt vinegar
1½ tablespoons tomato ketchup (sauce)
3 teaspoons cornflour
155 ml (5 fl oz/⅔ cup) chicken stock

Heat oil in a saucepan. Add onion, carrot, green pepper (capsicum) and ginger and stir-fry for 3 minutes. Add five-spice powder and remove from heat. Drain pineapple slices, reserving juice. Make juice up to 155 ml (5 fl oz/⅔ cup) with water. Cut 2 slices of pineapple into thin pieces (use the remaining pineapple in a fruit salad).

In a bowl, mix together sugar, soy sauce, sherry, vinegar, tomato ketchup (sauce) and pineapple juice. Add to pan together with pineapple pieces. Blend cornflour smoothly with a little stock. Add to pan and bring to the boil, stirring all the time. Reduce heat and simmer for 2 minutes, stirring. Serve hot with fried chicken, pork steaks or shellfish.

Makes 625 ml (20 fl oz/2½ cups).

Note: Garnish with a few pineapple leaves if they are available.

PICCALILLI

YOGURT TOMATO COOLER

125 g (4 oz) French green beans, topped and tailed and
    cut into 2.5 cm (1 in) pieces
250 g (8 oz) cauliflower flowerets
250 g (8 oz) small pickling onions, peeled
250 g (8 oz) piece cucumber, diced
125 g (4 oz/½ cup) cooking salt
1 teaspoon turmeric
3 teaspoons dry mustard
½ teaspoon ground ginger
90 g (3 oz/⅓ cup) granulated sugar
470 ml (15 fl oz/1¾ cups) distilled malt vinegar
4 teaspoons cornflour
cucumber, to garnish

Layer all vegetables in a colander with salt.

1 tablespoon corn oil
2 cloves garlic, crushed
½ teaspoon cumin seeds
220 ml (7 fl oz/1 cup) natural yogurt
½ teaspoon paprika
2 firm tomatoes, finely chopped
4 spring onions, finely chopped
2 tablespoons chopped fresh mint
salt and pepper
sprigs of mint, to garnish
hot buttered nan or pitta bread, to serve

Heat oil in a small saucepan. Add garlic and
cumin seeds and cook very gently for 2
minutes. Remove from heat and cool.

Leave to stand overnight. Rinse well under
cold running water and drain thoroughly.
Mix turmeric, mustard, ginger and sugar with
all but 60 ml (2 fl oz/¼ cup) vinegar and
blend well. Put mixture into a saucepan and
add vegetables. Simmer gently for 9-10
minutes until vegetables are part-cooked but
still crisp.

Put yogurt into a bowl. Add cooled garlic
mixture and paprika and stir well. Add
tomatoes, spring onions and chopped mint
and season with salt and pepper.

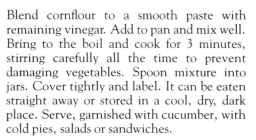

Blend cornflour to a smooth paste with
remaining vinegar. Add to pan and mix well.
Bring to the boil and cook for 3 minutes,
stirring carefully all the time to prevent
damaging vegetables. Spoon mixture into
jars. Cover tightly and label. It can be eaten
straight away or stored in a cool, dry, dark
place. Serve, garnished with cucumber, with
cold pies, salads or sandwiches.

Makes 1.5 kg (3 lb).

Turn mixture into a serving bowl and chill for
several hours before serving, garnished with
sprigs of fresh mint. Serve as an
accompaniment to curries or as a tasty snack
with hot buttered nan or pitta bread.

Serves 4.

Variation: Omit tomatoes. Add 1 peeled,
seeded and finely chopped, or grated,
cucumber to the mixture instead.

PICKLED RED CABBAGE

1 kg (2 lb) red cabbage
45 g (1½ oz/9 teaspoons) cooking salt
2 tablespoons Pickling Spice, see page 8
1.2 litres (40 fl oz/5 cups) distilled malt vinegar
2 teaspoons caraway seeds

Cut cabbage in fourths and discard center stalk. Shred cabbage finely. Layer in a colander with salt and let stand overnight.

Put Pickling Spice and vinegar into a saucepan. Bring to a boil and boil 3 minutes. Remove from heat and cool. When cool, strain and reserve liquid. Meanwhile, wash 4 pint jars in hot soapy water; rinse. Keep hot until needed. Prepare lids as manufacturer directs.

Rinse cabbage well under cold running water. Drain thoroughly and mix with caraway seeds. Pack cabbage into hot jars. Pour cold spiced vinegar over cabbage to cover completely. Wipe rims of jars with a clean damp cloth. Attach lids and place in canner. Process 10 minutes in a boiling-water bath. Store in a cool dry dark place at least 5 days before serving. Makes about 4 pint jars.

NOTE: Use cabbage within 2 months; if left longer cabbage loses its crispness. Garnish with an Italian parsley sprig, if desired, and serve as an accompaniment to cold meats and poultry.

SPICY PICKLED PLUMS

1 kg (2 lb) firm ripe plums
4 allspice berries
4 small dried red chillies
four 2.5 cm (1 in) cinnamon sticks
6 whole cloves
4 blades of mace
785 ml (25 fl oz/3 cups) distilled malt vinegar
750 g (1½ lb/3 cups) granulated sugar
sprig of mint, to garnish

Prick plums several times with a cocktail stick. Half-fill two 1 kg (2 lb) jars with plums.

Add 2 allspice berries, 2 chillies, 2 cinnamon sticks, 3 cloves and 2 blades mace to each jar. Add remaining plums to fill jars. Put vinegar and sugar into a saucepan and bring to the boil, stirring to dissolve sugar. Boil for 5 minutes.

Pour hot vinegar into jars to cover plums. Cool, then cover tightly and label. Store in a cool, dry, dark place for at least 1 month before serving. Serve, garnished with sprig of mint, with cold meats and salads.

Makes 2 kg (4 lb).

WINE-GLAZED ORANGES

PINEAPPLE CREAM PEARS

125 g (4oz/½ cup) granulated sugar
185 ml (6 fl oz/¾ cup) red wine
4 whole cloves
2 teaspoons cassia bark, broken into small pieces
1 small piece dried root ginger
4 large oranges
grated orange peel, to decorate
single (light) cream, to serve

Put sugar and 185 ml (6 fl oz/¾ cup) water into a saucepan and heat slowly, stirring to dissolve sugar. Add wine, cloves, cassia and ginger. Bring to the boil and boil until mixture is slightly thickened and syrupy. Cool for 5 minutes.

Meanwhile, prepare oranges. Peel oranges, using a sharp knife, removing all bitter white pith. Cut oranges into 0.5 cm (¼ in) thick slices and place in a shallow dish. Strain wine syrup over oranges. Cover and chill for several hours or overnight, turning slices occasionally in syrup.

Using cocktail sticks, secure orange slices together to form neat, whole oranges and place in a serving dish. Pour wine syrup over oranges. Decorate with orange peel and serve with cream.

Serves 4.

Note: If preferred, serve oranges in slices rather than as whole oranges.

1 tablespoon lemon juice
4 large, firm pears
4 pieces crystallized ginger, halved
30 g (1 oz/6 teaspoons) butter
1 tablespoon light soft brown sugar
155 ml (5 fl oz/⅔ cup) pineapple juice
155 ml (5 fl oz/⅔ cup) double (thick) cream
toasted, flaked almonds and fresh bay leaves, to decorate

Preheat oven to 190C (375F/Gas 5). Fill a bowl with cold water and add lemon juice. Peel and halve the pears. Cut away stalks and remove cores, using a teaspoon. Place prepared pears in bowl of lemon water.

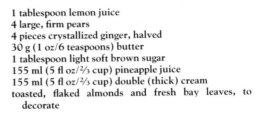

Lightly grease a shallow ovenproof dish. Pat pears dry on absorbent kitchen paper. Put a piece of crystallized ginger into the 'well' of each pear half. Arrange pears, cut-sides down, in the ovenproof dish.

Put butter into a saucepan with sugar and pineapple juice and heat gently to dissolve sugar. Add cream and boil for 5 minutes. Pour sauce over pears. Cover and bake in oven for 1 hour until pears are tender and sauce has thickened. Baste pears with sauce several times during cooking. Arrange pears on a warm serving plate and spoon sauce over. Decorate with toasted, flaked almonds and bay leaves to represent pear leaves. Serve hot.

Serves 4.

MELON & GINGER BASKET

1 large, ripe Honeydew melon
60 ml (2 fl oz/¼ cup) orange juice
1-2 pieces stem ginger, thinly sliced
2 tablespoons stem ginger syrup
freshly grated nutmeg
2 kiwi fruit, peeled, halved and sliced
8 lychees, peeled and stones removed
8 strawberries, halved
8 black grapes, halved and pips removed
ice cream, to serve
sprig of mint, to decorate

Cut a thin slice off one of the rounded sides of melon (not pointed ends), so melon will stand level on serving plate.

Make 2 cuts on either side of a central strip, to form a handle, about 2 cm (¾ in) wide. Continue cutting halfway down melon then cut from base of handle around either side of fruit so these two wedges can be lifted away to form a basket shape. Cut away flesh from inside the handle. Remove seeds from melon. Using a small melon scoop, scoop out flesh in neat balls and place in a bowl. (Alternatively, cut flesh into neat pieces.) Neaten edge of melon basket.

Add orange juice, sliced stem ginger and syrup and nutmeg to taste to melon balls and stir lightly. Add kiwi fruit, lychees, strawberries and grapes and mix lightly together. Spoon mixture into melon and pile fruits up attractively. Cover and chill before serving with ice cream. Decorate with mint.

Serves 4-6.

Variation: Use any fresh fruits of your choice, such as cherries, pineapple, peaches, figs, nectarines.

LEMON GINGER SYLLABUBS

315 ml (10 fl oz/1¼ cups) double (thick) cream
90 g (3 oz/⅓ cup) caster sugar
finely grated peel of 1 lemon
2 tablespoons lemon juice
2 pieces stem ginger, chopped
1 egg white
2 kiwi fruit, peeled, quartered and sliced
4 teaspoons stem ginger syrup
twists of lemon and slices stem ginger, to decorate
dainty sweet biscuits, to serve

Whip cream with sugar until it begins to thicken. Add lemon peel and juice and whisk until thick and velvety.

Fold in chopped stem ginger. Whisk egg white stiffly and fold into cream mixture. Place kiwi fruit in bases of 4 glasses. Sprinkle each one with stem ginger syrup. Top with cream mixture. Chill for 2 hours.

Decorate each one with a twist of lemon and slices of stem ginger. Serve with dainty sweet biscuits.

Serves 4.

Variation: Stoned cherries, sliced peaches or nectarines may be used instead of kiwi fruit, if preferred.

BERRIES & PEPPER SAUCE

1 lemon
250 g (8 oz/1 cup) granulated sugar
315 ml (10 fl oz/1¼ cups) orange juice
1 tablespoon green peppercorns, coarsely crushed
500 g (1 lb) strawberries
strawberry or mint leaves, to decorate, if desired
single (light) cream, to serve

Finely grate peel from lemon and put into a saucepan. Squeeze juice from lemon and reserve. Add sugar and 155 ml (5 fl oz/⅔ cup) water to pan and heat gently, stirring until sugar dissolves.

Bring to the boil and boil until syrup turns a light caramel colour. Remove from heat and, holding pan handle with a cloth (as mixture will splutter), add orange and lemon juices. Heat gently, stirring to dissolve caramel.

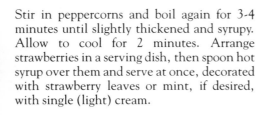

Stir in peppercorns and boil again for 3-4 minutes until slightly thickened and syrupy. Allow to cool for 2 minutes. Arrange strawberries in a serving dish, then spoon hot syrup over them and serve at once, decorated with strawberry leaves or mint, if desired, with single (light) cream.

Serves 4.

GLAZED APPLE TART

185 g (6 oz/1½ cups) plain flour
pinch of salt
140 g (4½ oz/½ cup plus 3 teaspoons) butter
3 tablespoons caster sugar
1 egg yolk
4 green eating apples (such as Granny Smith)
finely grated peel of ½ a lemon
½ teaspoon cornflour
½ teaspoon ground cinnamon
2 pinches of ground nutmeg
5 tablespoons apricot jam
2 tablespoons lemon juice
sprig of mint, to decorate
cream, to serve

Sift flour and salt into a bowl.

Add 125 g (4 oz/½ cup) butter and rub in finely until mixture resembles breadcrumbs. Stir in 1 tablespoon caster sugar and bind together with egg yolk and 2 teaspoons cold water. Knead gently until smooth and chill for 15 minutes. Preheat oven to 190C (375F/Gas 5). Melt remaining butter and use to grease a 20 cm (8 in) shallow sandwich cake tin. Sprinkle with remaining caster sugar. Peel, core and cut apples into fairly thin slices. Arrange a layer of apple slices in overlapping circles over base of tin.

Mix remaining slices with lemon peel, cornflour and spices. Pack on top of arranged slices. Roll out pastry to a round large enough to cover surface and fit into tin. Prick with a fork. Bake in oven for 40 minutes until pastry is golden brown. Carefully turn out onto a warm serving plate. Put jam and lemon juice into a saucepan and heat gently until melted, stirring. Spoon over apple. Serve hot or cold, decorated with a sprig of mint, with cream.

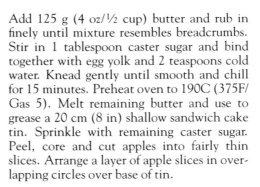

Serves 6-8.

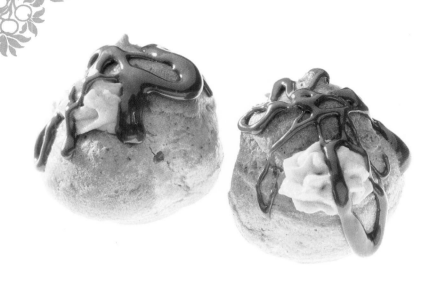

SPICY PROFITEROLES

75 g (2½ oz/½ cup, plus 6 teaspoons) plain flour
1 teaspoon ground cinnamon
67 g(2¼ oz/¼ cup, plus 1½ teaspoons) butter, diced
2 eggs, beaten
315 ml (10 fl oz/1¼ cups) double (thick) cream
1 tablespoon icing sugar
2 teaspoons coffee essence
125 g (4 oz) plain (dark) chocolate, broken up
2 tablespoons Tia Maria
2 tablespoons golden syrup
2 teaspoons caster sugar

Preheat oven to 200C (400F/Gas 6). Lightly grease 2 baking sheets.

Sift flour and ½ teaspoon cinnamon onto a piece of greaseproof paper. Put 155 ml (5 fl oz/⅔ cup) water in a saucepan. Add 52 g (1¾ oz/10½ teaspoons) butter and heat gently until butter melts. Do not allow water to boil before butter melts. Rapidly bring to boil, remove from heat and add flour all at once and stir quickly, using a wooden spoon, to form a smooth mixture. Return pan to medium heat for a few seconds and beat well until dough forms a smooth ball and leaves sides of pan clean.

Remove from heat and cool slightly. Gradually add beaten egg, a little at a time, beating well after each addition to form a smooth, shiny dough. Transfer dough to a piping bag fitted with a 2 cm (¾ in) plain nozzle. Pipe 24 small balls onto baking sheets.

Bake in the oven for 20 minutes, then reduce oven temperature to 180C (350F/Gas 4) and continue cooking for a further 15-20 minutes until buns are well risen, crisp and sound hollow when tapped on bases. Make a slit in the side of each one to allow steam to escape. Cool on a wire rack.

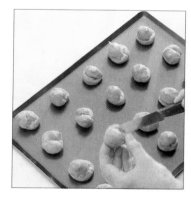

Whip cream with icing sugar and coffee essence until thick. Transfer to a piping bag fitted with a small star nozzle and pipe cream into choux buns. (Alternatively, use a teaspoon to fill buns with cream.) Arrange profiteroles in a pyramid-shape on a serving dish.

Melt chocolate and remaining butter in the top of a double boiler or a bowl set over a pan of simmering water. Stir in Tia Maria and syrup and continue stirring until sauce is smooth and coats back of a spoon. Spoon sauce over profiteroles and leave to set for a few minutes. Mix remaining cinnamon with caster sugar and sprinkle over profiteroles.

Serves 6.

BAKLAVA

60 g (2 oz/¼ cup) caster sugar
155 g (5 oz/1⅓ cups) blanched chopped almonds
90 g (3 oz/¾ cup) chopped walnuts
1½ teaspoons ground cinnamon
½ teaspoon Mixed Spice, see page 8
500 g (1 lb) filo pastry
200 g (7 oz/1 cup) unsalted butter, melted
220 g (12 oz/1½ cups) granulated sugar
4 large pieces cassia bark
6 whole cloves
strip of lemon peel
2 tablespoons clear honey

In a bowl, mix together caster sugar, almonds, walnuts, cinnamon and spice.

Preheat oven to 160C (325F/Gas 3). Grease a 25 x 32.5 cm (10 x 13 in) roasting tin. Line base with a sheet of filo pastry, trimming it to fit. Brush with melted butter and add a further 7 sheets of filo pastry, trimming and brushing each one with butter. Sprinkle over half nut mixture, then cover with 4 sheets pastry, trimming and brushing each one with melted butter. Sprinkle remaining nut mixture on top and cover with 5 more sheets of filo, trimming and brushing each one with melted butter. Spread any remaining butter on top.

Using a sharp knife, cut through top layers of pastry to make about 25 diamond-shaped pieces. Bake in oven for 1 hour until golden brown, covering with foil, if necessary, to prevent overbrowning. Leave to cool in tin. Put granulated sugar and 345 ml (11 fl oz/1⅓ cups) water in a large saucepan. Add cassia, cloves, lemon peel and honey and heat gently, stirring. Boil for 5 minutes, then strain over baklava. Leave overnight.

Makes about 25 pieces.

CORNISH SAFFRON CAKE

three 0.05 g packets saffron strands
1 tablespoon boiling water
90 g (3 oz/⅓ cup) caster sugar
250 ml (8 fl oz/1 cup) hand-hot water
3 teaspoons dried yeast
750 g (1½ lb/5 cups) strong plain white flour
¼ teaspoon salt
185 g (6 oz/¾ cup) lard
125 g (4 oz/½ cup) butter
250 g (8 oz/1⅔ cups) currants

Put a piece of foil in grill pan. Place saffron on foil and spread thinly. Switch grill to low and gently dry saffron (do not discolour) for 3-4 minutes.

Place saffron in a small bowl and crush to a fine powder. Add 1 tablespoon boiling water and leave to soak for 8 hours. Next day, dissolve 1 teaspoon of caster sugar in 60 ml (2 fl oz/¼ cup) of hand-hot water. Add yeast, whisk and leave for 10-15 minutes until frothy. Put flour, salt, lard and butter into a bowl and rub in finely. Mix in remaining sugar and currants. Stir saffron into remaining water and add to bowl. Stir in yeast and mix to form a dough. Knead lightly, then cover and leave in a warm place to rise until doubled in bulk.

Lightly grease two 1 kg (2lb) loaf tins. Knead dough and divide in half. Press each piece to a rectangle. Roll up and put into tins with joins underneath. Press into corners. Cover and prove at room temperature until risen to top of tins (this may take 2-3 hours). Preheat oven to 190C (375F/Gas 5). Bake in oven 35-45 minutes until cooked. Cover with foil if necessary, to prevent overbrowning. Cool on wire rack. Leave until the next day before slicing.

Makes 2 cakes.

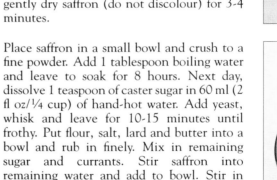

FROSTED GINGERBREAD

250 g (8 oz/2 cups) plain flour
¼ teaspoon salt
½ teaspoon Mixed Spice, see page 8
1½ teaspoons ground ginger
1 teaspoon bicarbonate of soda
90 g (3 oz/¼ cup) golden syrup
90 g (3 oz/¼ cup) black treacle
90 g (3 oz/⅓ cup) block margarine
90 g (3 oz/½ cup) dark soft brown sugar
2 eggs, beaten
220 ml (7 fl oz/1 cup) milk
90 g (3 oz) full fat soft cheese
185 g (6 oz/1 cup) icing sugar
slices of crystallized ginger, to decorate

JAMAICAN RUM CAKE

185 g (6 oz/1½ cups) self-raising flour
1½ teaspoons baking powder
1 teaspoon Mixed Spice, see page 8
185 g (6 oz/¾ cup) soft tub margarine
3 eggs
185 g (6 oz/¾ cup) caster sugar
6 teaspoons cocoa powder
6 teaspoons hot water
125 g (4 oz/½ cup) granulated sugar
2 cinnamon sticks
4 tablespoons dark rum
15 g (½ oz/6 teaspoons) slivered almonds
185 g (6 oz) plain (dark) chocolate, broken up
whipped cream

Preheat oven to 160C (325F/Gas 3).

Preheat oven to 160C (325F/Gas 3). Grease an 18 x 28 cm (7 x 11 in) shallow baking tin and line base with greased, greaseproof paper, allowing paper to stand 2.5 cm (1 in) above sides of tin. Sift flour, salt, mixed spice, ginger and bicarbonate of soda into a bowl. Put golden syrup, black treacle, margarine and brown sugar into a saucepan and heat gently until melted. Stir mixture into bowl and add eggs and milk. Stir well together until evenly mixed.

Well grease a 1.2 litre (40 fl oz/5 cup) fluted or plain ring tin and dust lightly with flour. Sift flour, baking powder and mixed spice into a bowl. Add margarine, and eggs and caster sugar. Blend cocoa with hot water and add to bowl. Beat well with wooden spoon for 2 minutes (or for only 1 minute, if using an electric mixer) until well blended. Turn mixture into prepared tin. Bake in oven for 1¼ hours or until well risen and beginning to shrink away from edge of tin. Carefully turn cake out onto a wire rack and leave to cool.

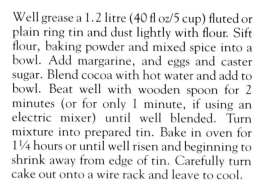

Pour into prepared tin and bake in the oven for 45-50 minutes until well risen and cooked through. Leave to cool in tin, then turn out and remove lining paper. In a bowl, soften cheese, then gradually sift in icing sugar. Mix well to make a soft creamy mixture. Spread over cold cake. Using blade of a knife, form a rippled effect on icing sugar. Decorate with crystallized ginger. Serve cut into chunky squares or slices.

Makes 12 squares or slices.

Put granulated sugar and 155 ml (5 fl oz/⅔ cup) water into a pan, add cinnamon and heat, stirring. Boil for 5 minutes. Remove from heat, add rum and discard cinnamon. Put cake on a plate. Spoon over syrup and leave for 2 hours. Stud top with almonds. Melt chocolate in the top of a double boiler or a bowl set over a pan of simmering water. Spoon chocolate over cake. Leave to set, then decorate around base of cake with piped, whipped cream.

Serves 10-12.

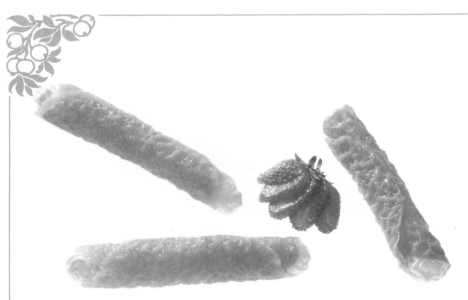

BRANDY SNAPS

60 g (2 oz/¼ cup) butter
60 g (2 oz/ ¼ cup) demerara sugar
60 g (2 oz/2 tablespoons) golden syrup
60 g (2 oz/½ cup) plain flour
pinch of salt
2 pinches of Mixed Spice, see page 8
½ teaspoon ground ginger
½ teaspoon lemon juice
155 ml (5 fl oz/⅔ cup) double (thick) cream
1 teaspoon icing sugar
few drops vanilla essence
small strawberries, sliced

Preheat oven to 160C (325F/Gas 3). Well grease 3 baking sheets.

Put butter, sugar and syrup into a saucepan and heat gently until butter has melted and sugar dissolved. Cool slightly. Sift flour, salt, mixed spice and ginger onto mixture, add lemon juice and stir well together. Put teaspoonfuls of mixture onto prepared baking sheets, spacing them well apart to allow for spreading. Bake in the oven (one sheet at a time) for 6-8 minutes until golden. Leave to cool on baking sheet for 2 minutes.

Using a palette knife, remove brandy snaps from baking sheet, one at a time, and roll around the handle of a wooden spoon. Leave to set before removing from handle. Just before serving, whip cream with icing sugar and vanilla essence until thick. Transfer cream to a piping bag fitted with a small star nozzle and pipe cream into the ends of each brandy snap. Add strawberry slices to each end and serve at once.

Makes 12.

GERMAN PEPPER COOKIES

1 egg
125 g (4 oz/½ cup) caster sugar
125 g (4 oz/1 cup) plain flour
pinch of salt
½ teaspoon ground cinnamon
¼ teaspoon ground white pepper
¼ teaspoon Mixed Spice, see page 8
3 teaspoons cornflour
½ teaspoon baking powder
finely grated peel of 1 lemon
2 tablespoons chopped mixed citrus peel
icing sugar for sprinkling

In a bowl, whisk egg and sugar together until light and fluffy.

Sift flour, salt, cinnamon, pepper, mixed spice, cornflour and baking powder onto mixture. Add lemon peel and mixed citrus peel and stir well together. Chill for 1 hour.

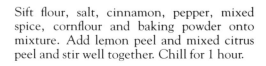

Preheat oven to 180C (350F/Gas 4). Lightly grease 2 or 3 baking sheets. Form mixture into 16 small balls and place, well apart on baking sheets. Bake in the oven for 20 minutes until well risen and lightly golden. Cool on a wire rack. Sprinkle with icing sugar. Store for several days before serving, to allow time for flavours to mellow.

Makes 16.

GLÜHWEIN

1 orange
8 whole cloves
60 g (2 oz/¼ cup) granulated sugar
3 cinnamon sticks
freshly grated nutmeg
3 blades of mace
1 litre (32 fl oz /4 cups) red wine
slices of orange and cinnamon sticks, to decorate

Stud orange with cloves and put into a saucepan. Add 315 ml (10 fl oz/ 1¼ cups) water, sugar, cinnamon, nutmeg to taste and mace.

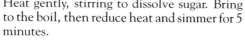

Heat gently, stirring to dissolve sugar. Bring to the boil, then reduce heat and simmer for 5 minutes.

Add red wine and heat through gently for a few minutes. Strain and serve hot in heatproof glasses. Float orange slices on top and decorate with cinnamon sticks.

Serves 8-10.

PINA COLADA PUNCH

1 piece dried root ginger, bruised with spoon
1 tablespoon light soft brown sugar
1 tablespoon cassia bark, broken into small pieces
2 China tea bags
60 g (2 oz/⅔ cup) desiccated coconut
315 ml (10 fl oz/1 ¼ cups) boiling water
470 ml (15 fl oz/1 ¾ cups) pineapple juice
155 ml (5 fl oz/⅔ cup) light rum or gin
cocktail cherries, pieces of pineapple and pineapple leaves, to decorate

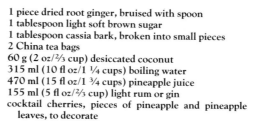

Put ginger, sugar and cassia bark into a saucepan.

Add 155 ml (5 fl oz/⅔ cup) water and bring to the boil. Cover and simmer for 5 minutes. Remove from heat and add tea bags. Leave to soak for 5 minutes, then strain into a bowl. Put coconut and boiling water into a blender or food processor and blend for 1 minute. Leave to stand for 5 minutes, then strain into tea mixture, pressing coconut well to extract all moisture.

Add pineapple juice and chill for 1 hour. Add rum or gin and stir well. Serve over crushed ice in tall glasses. Decorate glasses with cocktail sticks threaded with cocktail cherries, pieces of pineapple and pineapple leaves. Add a swizzle stick to each glass.

Serves 4-6.

Variation: Add more rum or gin for a stronger flavoured drink.

NEGUS

1 bottle ruby port
1 tablespoon light soft brown sugar
finely grated peel of 1 lemon
4 tablespoons lemon juice
¼ teaspoon freshly grated nutmeg
¼ teaspoon ground cinnamon
4 whole cloves
625 ml (20 fl oz/2½ cups) boiling water
thin strips of lemon peel, to decorate

Put port into a saucepan and heat gently (do not allow to boil).

Add sugar, grated lemon peel and juice and spices. Stir well together and leave over a very low heat for 10 minutes. Remove cloves.

Add boiling water and serve hot in heatproof glasses, decorated with strips of lemon peel.

Serves 10-12.

HOT MULLED CIDER

1 large cooking apple
14 whole cloves
3 cinnamon sticks
6 allspice berries
¼ teaspoon freshly grated nutmeg
30 g (1 oz/2 tablespoons) light soft brown sugar
1 litre (32 fl oz/4 cups) medium dry cider
30 g (1 oz/6 teaspoons) butter
slices of red apple and sprigs of mint, to decorate

Stud apple with cloves. Cut apple in half and put, cut-sides down, into a saucepan. Add 155 ml (5 fl oz/⅔ cup) water, cinnamon, allspice, nutmeg and sugar.

Cover and simmer gently for 20 minutes. Strain into a pan. Remove spices and press cooked apple through sieve into pan.

Add cider and butter and heat through gently. Serve hot in heatproof glasses with slices of red apple floating on top and decorated with sprigs of mint.

Serves 8-10.

GINGER BEER —  SHERBET

finely grated peel and juice of 1 large lemon
5 teaspoons cream of tartar
500 g (1 lb/2 cups) granulated sugar
30 g (1 oz) fresh root ginger, peeled
30 g (1 oz) dried root ginger
2.25 litres (4 pints/10 cups) boiling water
15 g (½ oz/3 teaspoons) fresh yeast
1 slice of toast
sprigs of mint, lemon slices and strips of peel,
    to decorate

Put lemon peel, cream of tartar and sugar into a large bowl or clean plastic bucket. Crush fresh ginger and dried root ginger with a rolling pin and add to bowl.

Pour over boiling water and stir well until sugar dissolves. Add 2.25 litres (4 pints/10 cups) cold water and lemon juice and stir well. Spread yeast on toast and float (yeast-side down) on mixture. Cover with a clean cloth and leave in a warm place for 24 hours.

Strain ginger beer through muslin. Pour into clean, plastic fizzy drink bottles, filling each one only half-full (this allows room for mixture to effervesce on opening). Screw on lids tightly and leave in a cool place for 2-3 days before drinking. (Even if the ginger beer is not required at this stage, it is a wise precaution to open each bottle to allow excess air to escape.) Once opened, drink within 2 weeks. Serve, decorated with sprigs of mint, lemon slices and strips of peel.

Serves 15-20.

250 g (8 oz/1 cup) granulated sugar
2 cinnamon sticks
½ teaspoon whole cloves
8 green cardamons, lightly crushed
3 strips of lemon peel
½ teaspoon rose water
1-2 drops red food colouring, if desired
curls of lemon peel and rose petals, to decorate

Put 470 ml (15 fl oz/1¾ cups) water into a saucepan. Add sugar, cinnamon, cloves, cardamons and strips of lemon peel. Heat gently, stirring to dissolve sugar.

Bring to the boil, then reduce heat and simmer gently for 20-30 minutes until mixture is thickened and syrupy. Remove from heat.

Stir in rose water and colouring, if desired. Strain and leave to cool, then dilute with ice-cold water. Serve in glasses, decorated with curls of lemon peel and rose petals.

Serves 6-8.

SWEET LASSI

AUSTRIAN CHOCOLATE CUP

470 ml (15 fl oz/1¾ cups) natural yogurt
4 ice cubes
315 ml (10 fl oz/1¼ cups) ice-cold water
2 teaspoons lemon juice
2 tablespoons caster sugar
ice cubes, to serve
½ teaspoon cumin seeds, crushed
thin slices of lemon and sprigs of mint, to decorate

Put yogurt, 4 ice cubes and ice-cold water into a blender or food processor and blend for 30 seconds.

90 g (3 oz) plain (dark) chocolate, broken up
finely grated peel of 1 small orange
¼ teaspoon ground cinnamon
375 ml (12 fl oz/1½ cups) milk
4 tablespoons double (thick) cream
grated chocolate, to serve
cinnamon sticks, to decorate

Put chocolate, orange peel, cinnamon and 3 tablespoons milk into a saucepan and heat very gently until melted, stirring frequently.

Add lemon juice and caster sugar and blend mixture again until thoroughly combined.

Add remaining milk and heat through gently until piping hot, stirring frequently. Whisk cream until softly peaking.

Pour mixture over ice cubes in 6 glasses and serve, sprinkled with crushed cumin seeds. Decorate each glass with a thin slice of lemon and a sprig of mint.

Serves 6.

Pour hot chocolate into mugs or heatproof glasses. Top each one with a spoonful of whipped cream. Sprinkle with grated chocolate and add a cinnamon stick to each one for stirring.

Serves 2-3.

Note: Wind a curly strip of orange peel around each cinnamon stick for a pretty effect.

CURRIES
AND
INDIAN FOOD

THE CULTURAL INFLUENCES

Indian food encompasses the cooking of many different regions – the country itself is huge, over a million square miles – and the foods are quite different from state to state.

In the north, where the climate is temperate, sheep are reared – and the lamb dishes are generally cooked slowly in the oven. Travelling south through Delhi and the Punjab, the diet becomes much richer – here they cook mainly with ghee (a clarified butter) and eat both goat and chicken. In these northern regions, instead of rice, the preference is for breads.

To the east, around the Bay of Bengal, there is an abundance of fish from the many rivers and, of course, from the bay itself. Coconut palms grow in the hot and humid climate, so coconuts feature strongly in many of their recipes. On the west coast, in Gujarat, the people are mainly vegetarian, eating pulses and vegetables, and in Tamil Nadu in the far south east, the people are also vegetarian.

The humid tropical conditions of the south west, in Goa and Malabar, mean that date and coconut palms,

and banana plants flourish and here there is also plenty of fish and shellfish. Southern Indians eat more rice than the northerners and they prefer to steam foods – the dishes are traditionally very hot, much more so than in the north. However, the story doesn't end there.

Influence of race and religion

India is a country of vastly varied races and religions – and it is religion that influences diet to the greatest extent. There are hundreds of different religions, some original, others imported over the centuries by conquering peoples from other lands, each with its own customs and taboos. For instance, Moslems and Jews don't eat pork, while Hindus and Sikhs are prohibited from eating beef, and although many Hindus are strict vegetarians, others eat fish and shellfish, classing these as a harvest from the seas.

Use of spices

The imaginative use of spices sets Indian cooking apart from other cuisines – it is by far the most aromatic of

all types of cooking – and perhaps the most pleasant discovery one can make about it is that although always spicy, the food isn't necessarily hot. In fact chillies – which make the food hot – were only introduced to India in the 16th century by Portuguese traders.

Red chillies are usually hotter than green and larger chillies generally milder than small ones, and unless you like very hot food, the seeds of all types are best removed. Be careful when handling the chillies, they contain an irritant which can burn, especially tender areas like the eyes and mouth. Try not to touch the seeds or cut surfaces of the chillies and always wash your hands afterwards.

Other spices can add warmth in different degrees – mustard seeds, black pepper and cayenne pepper are all quite hot, while ground ginger, nutmeg and cardamom are warm. Whole spices are best removed from dishes before serving.

The cornerstone of Indian cooking is the spice mixtures – or masalas. Spices release their flavour when they are crushed and traditionally spices are

ground by hand on a hard grinding stone with a pestle. At home, a mortar and pestle works very well for small quantities. However, if you have an electric coffee grinder, you will be able to make light work of spice grinding.

The most common spices are cumin, coriander and mustard seeds, black pepper, ground turmeric, cinnamon, cardamom and cloves. It's worth going to a specialist shop to buy whole spices rather than using the ready-ground ones as the whole spices have a stronger flavour which lasts much longer. Buy small quantities and store them in an airtight container.

Fats

The fats traditionally used in Indian cooking are ghee (a clarified butter) and solid vegetable fat. Until recently in Northern India ghee was the only fat used, however, there is a growing awareness about healthy eating and many Indians are swapping to vegetable fat. I have used vegetable oil in most of the recipes and have generally reduced fat quantities where I felt it would improve the taste of the recipe.

SPICE MIXES & COCONUT MILK

NUT MASALA

2 tablespoons vegetable oil
1 teaspoon cumin seeds
1 teaspoon cardamom seeds
3 teaspoons poppy seeds
1 teaspoon black peppercorns
2 cloves garlic, crushed
2.5 cm (1 in) piece fresh root ginger, grated
60 g (2 oz/⅓ cup) blanched almonds or unsalted
    cashew nuts, chopped
75 ml (2½ fl oz/⅓ cup) boiling water

Heat oil in a heavy-based frying pan, add spices and fry over a medium heat for 5-10 minutes, until golden brown, stirring constantly. Add garlic and ginger and cook for 2 minutes more, then leave to cool. Put spice mixture in a blender or food processor fitted with a metal blade. Add almonds or cashew nuts and water and grind to a smooth paste. Cover tightly and keep in a cool place for up to 1 week.

TANDOORI MASALA

3 teaspoons cumin seeds
3 teaspoons coriander seeds
3 teaspoons cayenne pepper
few drops red food colouring

Grind cumin and coriander seeds using a coffee grinder or pestle and mortar. Stir in cayenne pepper and food colouring and mix well. Store in a small, airtight jar for up to 2 months.

MURGHAL MASALA

seeds from 60 g (2 oz) green cardamom pods
two 7.5 cm (3 in) cinnamon sticks, crushed
3 teaspoons whole cloves
3 teaspoons black peppercorns
1 teaspoon grated nutmeg

Grind spices to a fine powder using a coffee grinder or pestle and mortar. Store in a small, airtight jar for up to 2 months.

GARAM MASALA

4 teaspoons cardamom seeds
two 7.5 cm (3 in) cinnamon sticks, crushed
2 teaspoons whole cloves
4 teaspoons black peppercorns
3 tablespoons cumin seeds
3 tablespoons coriander seeds

Put spices in a heavy-based frying pan and fry over medium heat for 5-10 minutes, until browned, stirring. Cool, then grind to a fine powder. Store for up to 2 months.

HOT SPICE MIX

4 tablespoons cumin seeds
8 dried red chillies
3 teaspoons black peppercorns
3 teaspoons cardamom seeds
7.5 cm (3 in) cinnamon stick, crushed
4 teaspoons black mustard seeds
3 teaspoons fenugreek seeds

Prepare as for Garam Masala (above). Store in an airtight jar for up to 2 months.

COCONUT MILK

100 g (3½ oz/1 cup) desiccated, fresh or creamed
    coconut
500 ml (16 fl oz/2 cups) hot water

Put coconut and water in a blender or food processor fitted with a metal blade; process for 1 minute. Strain through a nylon sieve, squeezing out liquid, then discard coconut. (There is no need to sieve creamed coconut.)

Makes about 500 ml (16 fl oz/2 cups).

MURGHAL MASALA CHOPS

8 best end-of-neck lamb chops
3 teaspoons Murghal Masala, see page 51
¼ teaspoon chilli powder
1 clove garlic, crushed
3 teaspoons lemon juice
curly endive and cherry tomatoes, to garnish

Wipe lamb chops and trim off any excess fat. Slash meaty parts 2 or 3 times on each side and set aside.

Put murghal masala, chilli powder, garlic and lemon juice in a small bowl and mix to a smooth paste. Rub paste into chops and leave them in a cool place for 2-3 hours to allow meat to absorb flavours.

Heat grill. Place chops on a grill rack and cook for 12-15 minutes, turning over half-way through cooking, until browned on outsides and just pink in centres. Press point of a sharp knife into centres of chops – when they are ready, juices will be just faintly pink. Serve hot, garnished with curly endive and tomatoes.

Serves 4.

SKEWERED BEEF KEBABS

750 g (1½ lb) lean minced beef
1 onion, finely chopped
5 cm (2 in) piece fresh root ginger, grated
3 cloves garlic, crushed
1 teaspoon chilli powder
3 teaspoons Garam Masala, see page 51
1 tablespoon chopped fresh coriander
3 teaspoons ground almonds
1 egg, beaten
30 g (1 oz/¼ cup) chick-pea flour
6 tablespoons natural yogurt
2 teaspoons vegetable oil
raw onion rings and thin lemon wedges, to garnish

In a large bowl, mix beef, onion, ginger, garlic, chilli powder, garam masala, coriander, almonds, egg and flour together. Cover beef mixture and leave in a cool place for up to 4 hours to allow flavours to blend. Shape into 16-20 long ovals and thread onto 4 long skewers. Mix together yogurt and oil and brush over kebabs.

Heat grill. Cook kebabs for 20-25 minutes, until well browned and no longer pink in centres. Baste kebabs with more of the yogurt and oil mixture and turn occasionally during cooking. Serve hot, garnished with onion rings and lemon wedges.

Serves 4.

Note: The meatball mixture can be made up to 12 hours in advance and stored in a refrigerator.

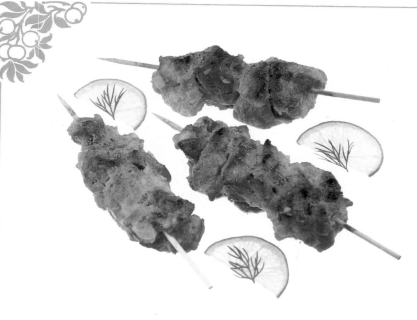

LAMB TIKKA

1 kg (2 lb) boneless leg of lamb
1 teaspoon ground cumin
¾ teaspoon turmeric
salt
6 tablespoons natural yogurt
½ small onion, finely chopped
5 cm (2 in) piece fresh root ginger, grated
2 cloves garlic, crushed
few drops red food colouring, optional
1 teaspoon Garam Masala, see page 51

Trim fat from lamb and cut lamb into 4 cm (1½ in) cubes. Put lamb in a bowl and add cumin, turmeric, salt, yogurt, onion, ginger and garlic.

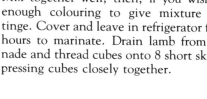

Mix together well, then, if you wish, add enough colouring to give mixture a red tinge. Cover and leave in refrigerator for 4-6 hours to marinate. Drain lamb from marinade and thread cubes onto 8 short skewers, pressing cubes closely together.

Heat grill. Cook kebabs for 15-20 minutes, basting kebabs with any remaining marinade and turning occasionally during cooking, until well browned and done to taste. Sprinkle with garam masala and serve at once.

Serves 4.

Note: These kebabs can be cooked on a barbecue using metal skewers. Cooking time depends on heat of barbecue.

KASHMIR MEATBALL CURRY

750 g (1½ lb) minced lamb
30 g (1 oz/¼ cup) chick-pea flour
9 teaspoons Garam Masala, see page 51
¼ teaspoon cayenne pepper
6 tablespoons natural yogurt
salt
2 tablespoons vegetable oil
7.5 cm (3 in) cinnamon stick
6 green cardamon pods, bruised
2 fresh bay leaves
6 whole cloves
5 cm (2 in) piece fresh root ginger, grated
2 tablespoons chopped fresh coriander, to garnish

Put lamb, flour, garam masala, cayenne and half the yogurt in a bowl. Season with salt and mix together well. Shape into 16 long ovals. Heat oil in a shallow heavy-based pan, add cinnamon, cardamom pods, bay leaves and cloves. Stir-fry for a few seconds, then add meatballs and fry until lightly browned on all sides. Add ginger and fry for a few seconds more. Stir remaining yogurt into 250 ml (8 fl oz/1 cup) cold water and pour over meatballs.

Cover pan and bring to the boil. Reduce heat and simmer for about 30 minutes, stirring gently 2 or 3 times, until meatballs are cooked and almost all the sauce has been absorbed. Sprinkle with coriander and serve at once.

Serves 4.

Note: If meatballs release a lot of fat during initial frying, drain it off before adding yogurt liquid.

LAMB KORMA

MADRAS MEAT CURRY

750 g (1½ lb) boneless leg of lamb
60 ml (2 fl oz/¼ cup) vegetable oil
1 large onion, finely chopped
1 quantity Cashew Nut Masala, see page 51
6 teaspoons Garam Masala, see page 51
3 dried red chillies, seeded and crushed
2.5 cm (1 in) piece fresh root ginger, grated
1 tablespoon chopped fresh coriander
250 ml (8 fl oz/1 cup) single (light) cream
salt
2 teaspoons lemon juice
coriander leaves and lemon wedges, to garnish

Wipe lamb, trim off excess fat and cut into 5 cm (2 in) cubes.

750 g (1½ lb) braising steak
6 teaspoons vegetable oil
1 large onion, finely sliced
4 cloves
4 green cardamom pods, bruised
3 fresh green chillies, seeded and finely chopped
2 dry red chillies, seeded and crushed
2.5 cm (1 in) piece fresh root ginger, grated
2 cloves garlic, crushed
2 teaspoons ground coriander
2 teaspoons turmeric
60 ml (2 fl oz/¼ cup) tamarind juice, see Note
salt
lettuce leaves, to garnish

Heat oil in a heavy-based pan, add lamb and fry until browned all over. Add onion and cook for about 5 minutes, stirring frequently, until soft. Stir in masalas, chillies and ginger and cook for 2 minutes more.

Cut beef into 2.5 cm (1 in) cubes. Heat oil in a large heavy-based pan, add beef and fry until browned all over. Remove with a slotted spoon and set aside. Add onion, cloves and cardamom pods to pan and fry for about 8 minutes, stirring, until onion is soft and golden brown. Stir in chillies, ginger, garlic, coriander and turmeric and fry for 2 minutes. Return beef to pan, add 60 ml (2 fl oz/¼ cup) water and simmer, covered, for 1 hour.

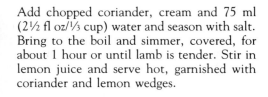

Add chopped coriander, cream and 75 ml (2½ fl oz/⅓ cup) water and season with salt. Bring to the boil and simmer, covered, for about 1 hour or until lamb is tender. Stir in lemon juice and serve hot, garnished with coriander and lemon wedges.

Serves 4.

Stir in tamarind juice and season with salt, re-cover and simmer, covered, for 15-30 minutes, until beef is tender. Serve garnished with lettuce leaves.

Serves 4.

Note: Tamarind pulp, available in Indian shops, is used to make tamarind juice. Soak walnut-sized piece in 250 ml (8 fl oz/1 cup) boiling water for 20 minutes, then squeeze pulp in muslin to extract juice; discard pulp.

LAMB WITH ONIONS

750 g (1½ lb) shoulder of lamb, boned
1 teaspoon turmeric
1 teaspoon ground cumin
1 teaspoon ground coriander
2.5 cm (1 in) piece fresh root ginger, grated
2 cloves garlic, crushed
45 ml (1½ fl oz/9 teaspoons) vegetable oil
3 teaspoons caster sugar
4 large onions, sliced into thin rings
500 g (1 lb) potatoes, cut into large chunks
salt and cayenne pepper
1 teaspoon Garam Masala, see page 51
rosemary sprigs, to garnish

Wipe lamb, trim and cut into cubes.

Put lamb in a glass or china bowl. Mix together turmeric, cumin, coriander, ginger and garlic and add to lamb. Stir well, then cover loosely and leave in a cool place for 2-3 hours. Heat oil in heavy-based pan until smoking. Stir in sugar, then add onions and cook over a medium to high heat for 10 minutes, stirring frequently, until a rich brown. Remove onions with a slotted spoon and set aside.

Add lamb to pan and fry until browned all over. Add potatoes and fry, stirring, for 2 minutes. Return onions to pan, add 250 ml (8 fl oz/1 cup) water and season with salt and cayenne pepper. Bring to the boil and simmer, covered, for 1¼ hours, or until lamb is tender, stirring occasionally. Stir in garam masala and serve, garnished with rosemary sprigs.

Serves 4.

LEG OF LAMB & PISTACHIOS

1.75-2 kg (3½-4 lb) leg of lamb, boned, rolled and tied
2 cloves garlic, crushed
2.5 cm (1 in) piece fresh root ginger, grated
1 teaspoon ground cumin
2 teaspoons Murgal Masala, see page 51
salt and cayenne pepper
125 g (4 oz/¾ cup) shelled pistachio nuts
6 teaspoons lemon juice
6 teaspoons soft brown sugar
125 ml (4 fl oz/½ cup) natural yogurt
2 pinches saffron threads
6 teaspoons boiling water
3 teaspoons cornflour
2 tablespoons shelled pistachio nuts, sliced, to garnish

Prick lamb all over with point of a knife and place in a large glass bowl. Put garlic, ginger, cumin, masala, salt and cayenne pepper to taste, pistachio nuts, lemon juice, sugar and yogurt in a blender or food processor fitted with a metal blade and process until smooth. Pour over lamb and leave to marinate for 24 hours, turning lamb occasionally. Preheat oven to 180C (350F/Gas 4). Transfer lamb to a flameproof casserole, add 155 ml (5 fl oz/⅔ cup) water and bring to the boil.

Cover tightly and cook in oven for 1½ hours. Reduce heat to 140C (275F/Gas 1) and cook for 30 minutes. Turn off oven and leave for 30 minutes. Soak saffron in water for 20 minutes, then blend in cornflour. Remove lamb and keep warm. Skim excess fat from sauce, add saffron mixture and boil, stirring, until thick. Slice lamb, pour a little sauce over; garnish with nuts. Serve rest of sauce separately.

Serves 6-8.

PORK IN SPINACH SAUCE

LAMB WITH CAULIFLOWER

750 g (1½ lb) fresh spinach, well rinsed
salt
750 g (1½ lb) lean boneless pork
3 tablespoons vegetable oil
2 onions, finely sliced
4 cloves garlic, crushed
2.5 cm (1 in) piece fresh root ginger, grated
9 teaspoons Garam Masala, see page 51
½ teaspoon turmeric
1 bay leaf
2 tomatoes, skinned and chopped
2 fresh green chillies, seeded and chopped
155 ml (5 fl oz/⅔ cup) natural yogurt
tomato slices and bay leaves, to garnish

750 g (1½ lb) lamb fillet
3 tablespoons vegetable oil
2 onions, finely chopped
2.5 cm (1 in) piece fresh root ginger, grated
4 cloves garlic, crushed
6 teaspoons Hot Spice Mix, see page 51
315 ml (10 fl oz/1¼ cups) lamb stock
salt
1 small cauliflower, cut into flowerets
1 teaspoon Garam Masala, see page 51
2 teaspoons lime juice
lime slices, to garnish

Trim excess fat from lamb and cut into 2.5 cm (1 in) cubes. Set aside.

Trim stems from spinach and cook leaves in boiling salted water for 2-3 minutes, until tender. Drain thoroughly and rinse under cold running water. Put in a blender or food processor fitted with a metal blade and process to a smooth purée. Set aside. Pre-heat oven to 160C (325F/Gas 3). Cut pork into 2.5 cm (1 in) cubes. Heat oil in a large frying pan and fry pork until browned all over. Transfer to a casserole using a slotted spoon.

Heat oil in a large heavy-based pan and add onions. Fry over a medium heat for 5 minutes, stirring frequently, until soft. Stir in ginger, garlic and hot spice mix and fry for 1 minute. Add lamb and fry until browned all over.

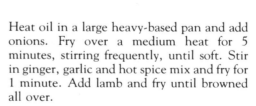

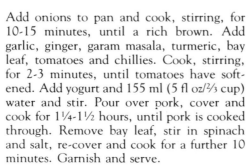

Add onions to pan and cook, stirring, for 10-15 minutes, until a rich brown. Add garlic, ginger, garam masala, turmeric, bay leaf, tomatoes and chillies. Cook, stirring, for 2-3 minutes, until tomatoes have soft-ened. Add yogurt and 155 ml (5 fl oz/⅔ cup) water and stir. Pour over pork, cover and cook for 1¼-1½ hours, until pork is cooked through. Remove bay leaf, stir in spinach and salt, re-cover and cook for a further 10 minutes. Garnish and serve.

Stir in stock, season with salt and bring to the boil, then simmer, covered, for 25 minutes. Add cauliflower and cook for a further 5-10 minutes, stirring occasionally, until lamb and cauliflower are tender. Sprinkle in garam masala and lime juice and stir gently. Serve the lamb hot, garnished with thin lime slices.

Serves 4.

Serves 4.

CHICKEN IN GINGER SAUCE

ROAST DUCK IN FRUIT SAUCE

four 185 g (6 oz) boneless chicken breasts (fillets), skinned
2 tablespoons vegetable oil
6 spring onions, finely chopped
3 cloves garlic, crushed
5 cm (2 in) piece fresh root ginger, grated
1 teaspoon ground cumin
2 teaspoons Garam Masala, see page 51
salt and pepper
3 teaspoons lemon juice
6 tablespoons hot water
parsley sprigs and lemon slices, to garnish

Wash chicken, pat dry with absorbent kitchen paper and slice thinly.

2.25 kg (4½ lb) duck
3 onions, chopped
125 g (4 oz/1 cup) chopped mixed nuts
60 g (2 oz/1 cup) fresh breadcrumbs
4 tablespoons chopped fresh coriander
salt and cayenne pepper
1 egg yolk
3 teaspoons Garam Masala, see page 51
2 tablespoons vegetable oil
2 garlic cloves, crushed
2.5 cm (1 in) piece fresh root ginger, grated
1 teaspoon turmeric
6 teaspoons ground coriander
1 teaspoon chick-pea flour
315 ml (10 fl oz/1¼ cups) natural yogurt
juice of 2 lemons and 2 oranges

Heat oil in a large frying pan, add onions and fry for 2-3 minutes, stirring, to soften. Remove from pan with a slotted spoon. Put chicken in pan and fry over a high heat, stirring frequently, for about 5 minutes or until browned all over.

Preheat oven to 190C (375F/Gas 5). Wash duck and pat dry with absorbent kitchen paper, then prick skin with a fork. In a bowl, mix 1 onion, nuts, breadcrumbs, 3 tablespoons fresh coriander, salt and cayenne pepper and yolk together. Use to stuff duck, then truss neatly. Rub garam masala into skin, place duck in a roasting tin and cook for 1¼ hours or until tender. Remove duck and keep warm. Heat oil in a saucepan, add remaining onions and cook, stirring, for 5 minutes, until soft.

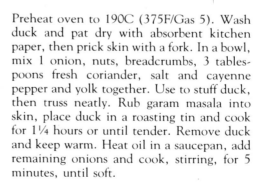

Stir in garlic, ginger, cumin and garam masala and season with salt and pepper. Cook for 1 minute, then stir in onions, lemon juice and water. Cover and cook over a low heat for about 10 minutes or until chicken is tender. Serve hot, garnished with parsley and lemon.

Serves 4.

Stir in garlic, ginger, turmeric, ground coriander, salt and cayenne pepper to taste and flour. Cook for 1 minute, then stir in yogurt. Simmer for 10 minutes, then stir in lemon and orange juices and heat gently, without boiling. Carve duck, pour over sauce and sprinkle with remaining coriander. Serve hot.

Serves 4.

Note: This looks very attractive garnished with spirals of lemon and orange peel.

LEMON & CORIANDER CHICKEN

— APRICOT & CHICKEN CURRY —

4 chicken thighs, skinned
4 chicken drumsticks, skinned
60 ml (2 fl oz/¼ cup) vegetable oil
5 cm (2 in) piece fresh root ginger, grated
4 cloves garlic, crushed
1 fresh green chilli, seeded and finely chopped
½ teaspoon turmeric
1 teaspoon ground cumin
1 teaspoon ground coriander
salt and cayenne pepper
grated peel and juice of 1 lemon
125 g (4 oz) fresh coriander leaves, chopped
coriander leaves and lemon slices, to garnish

1.25 kg (2½ lb) chicken joints, skinned
½ teaspoon chilli powder
3 teaspoons Garam Masala, see page 51
2.5 cm (1 in) piece fresh root ginger, grated
2 cloves garlic, crushed
125 g (4 oz/1 cup) ready-to-eat dried apricots
2 tablespoons vegetable oil
2 onions, finely sliced
440 g (14 oz) can chopped tomatoes
3 teaspoons sugar
6 teaspoons white wine vinegar
salt

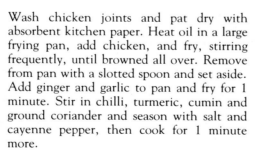

Wash chicken joints and pat dry with absorbent kitchen paper. Heat oil in a large frying pan, add chicken, and fry, stirring frequently, until browned all over. Remove from pan with a slotted spoon and set aside. Add ginger and garlic to pan and fry for 1 minute. Stir in chilli, turmeric, cumin and ground coriander and season with salt and cayenne pepper, then cook for 1 minute more.

Wash chicken and pat dry with absorbent kitchen paper. Cut each joint into 4 pieces and put in a large bowl. Add chilli powder, garam masala, ginger and garlic and toss well to coat chicken pieces. Cover and leave in a cool place for 2-3 hours, to allow chicken to absorb flavours. In a separate bowl, put apricots and 155 ml (5 fl oz/⅔ cup) water and leave to soak for 2-3 hours.

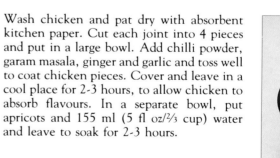

Return chicken to pan, add 125 ml (4 fl oz/½ cup) water and lemon peel and juice. Bring to the boil, then cover and cook over a medium heat for 25-30 minutes or until chicken is tender. Stir in chopped coriander, then serve hot, garnished with fresh coriander leaves and lemon slices.

Serves 4.

Variation: Use fresh parsley, or parsley and mint, instead of coriander, if preferred.

Heat oil in a large heavy-based pan and add chicken. Fry over a high heat for 5 minutes or until browned all over. Remove from pan and set aside. Add onions to pan and cook, stirring, for about 5 minutes, until soft. Return chicken to pan with tomatoes and cook, covered, over a low heat for 20 minutes. Drain apricots, add to pan with sugar and vinegar. Season with salt. Simmer, covered, for 10-15 minutes. Serve hot.

Serves 4.

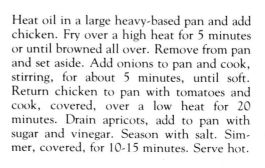

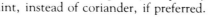

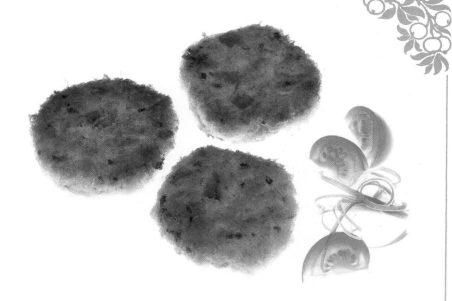

TANDOORI CHICKEN

1.25 kg (2½ lb) chicken joints, skinned
3 teaspoons lime juice
salt
1 small onion
3 teaspoons Tandoori Masala, see page 51
2 teaspoons Garam Masala, see page 51
2.5 cm (1 in) piece fresh root ginger, grated
315 ml (10 fl oz/1¼ cups) natural yogurt
lime wedges and coriander leaves, to garnish

Wash chicken joints and pat dry with absorbent kitchen paper, then slash meaty parts 2 or 3 times.

Place chicken in a shallow non-metal dish. Sprinkle with lime juice and salt and set aside. Put onion, masalas, ginger, salt and yogurt into a blender or food processor fitted with a metal blade and process until smooth and frothy. Pour over chicken and cover loosely. Leave to marinate in a cool place for 6 hours or overnight.

Preheat oven to 200C (400F/Gas 6). Drain excess marinade from chicken joints and place them in a roasting tin. Cook for 25-30 minutes, until tender and well browned. Serve hot, garnished with lime wedges and coriander leaves.

Serves 4.

Note: If preferred, use a whole 1.5 kg (3 lb) roasting chicken and cook for 1¼-1½ hours or until juices run clear.

SPICY CHICKEN PATTIES

625 g (1¼ lb) boneless chicken breasts (fillets), skinned
90 g (3 oz/1½ cups) fresh breadcrumbs
4 spring onions, finely chopped
3 tomatoes, skinned, seeded and chopped
3 tablespoons chopped fresh coriander
2.5 cm (1 in) piece fresh root ginger, grated
1 clove garlic, crushed
1 teaspoon ground cumin
1 teaspoon Garam Masala, see page 51
salt and cayenne pepper
1 egg, beaten
60 ml (2 fl oz/¼ cup) vegetable oil
tomato wedges and spring onion tassels, to garnish

Wash chicken breasts (fillets) and pat dry with absorbent kitchen paper. Finely mince chicken and put into a large bowl with half the breadcrumbs and the onions, tomatoes, coriander, ginger, garlic, cumin, garam masala, salt and cayenne pepper to taste, and egg. Mix thoroughly, then divide into 18 pieces and form into patties. Roll patties in remaining breadcrumbs to coat all over.

Heat oil in a large frying pan. Fry patties in 2 or 3 batches for 10-12 minutes, until crisp and golden brown on both sides and no longer pink in centres. Drain on absorbent kitchen paper. Serve hot, garnished with tomato wedges and spring onion tassels.

Serves 6.

Note: Patties can be prepared up to 12 hours in advance and chilled.

DUCK & COCONUT CURRY

CHICKEN BIRYANI

4 duck portions, skinned
2 tablespoons vegetable oil
1 teaspoon mustard seeds
1 onion, finely chopped
3 cloves garlic, crushed
5 cm (2 in) piece fresh root ginger, grated
2 fresh green chillies, seeded and chopped
1 teaspoon ground cumin
3 teaspoons ground coriander
1 teaspoon turmeric
3 teaspoons white wine vinegar
salt and cayenne pepper
315 ml (10 fl oz/1¼ cups) Coconut Milk, see page 51
2 tablespoons shredded coconut, toasted, and lemon
    wedges, to garnish

625 g (1¼ lb) boneless chicken breasts (fillets),
    skinned
500 g (1 lb/3 cups) basmati rice, washed
6 tablespoons vegetable oil
6 green cardamom pods, bruised
½ teaspoon cumin seeds
2 onions, finely sliced
4 cloves garlic, crushed
5 cm (2 in) piece fresh root ginger, grated
155 ml (5 fl oz/⅔ cup) natural yogurt
salt and pepper
large pinch saffron threads
6 teaspoons boiling water
few drops red food colouring
3 tablespoons flaked almonds, toasted, and
    2 tablespoons sultanas, to garnish

Wash duck and pat dry with absorbent kitchen paper. Heat oil in a large frying pan, add duck and fry, stirring, over a high heat for 8-10 minutes, until browned all over, then remove from pan. Pour off all but 2 tablespoons fat from pan, add mustard seeds and fry for 1 minute or until they begin to pop.

Cut chicken into 2 cm (¾ in) cubes. Set aside. Soak rice in cold water for 30 minutes, then drain. Heat 60 ml (2 fl oz/¼ cup) oil in a large heavy-based pan, add cardamom pods and cumin seeds and fry for 1 minute. Stir in onions, garlic, ginger and chicken and cook for about 5 minutes, stirring, over a high heat until chicken is browned all over. Stir in yogurt 1 tablespoon at a time, then add 125 ml (4 fl oz/½ cup) water. Cover and simmer for 15 minutes.

Add onion to pan and cook, stirring, over a medium heat for 8 minutes or until soft and golden. Stir in garlic, ginger, chillies, cumin, coriander and turmeric and fry for 2 minutes. Stir in vinegar and season with salt and cayenne pepper. Return duck to pan and turn pieces to coat them in spice mixture. Stir in coconut milk and bring to the boil. Cover and cook over a low heat for about 40 minutes or until duck is tender. Garnish and serve hot.

Heat remaining oil in separate pan, stir in rice and fry for 2-3 minutes, until golden, stirring all the time. Stir into chicken mixture and season with salt and pepper. Cover and simmer for 12-15 minutes, until rice and chicken are tender. Soak saffron in boiling water for 5 minutes. Add 6 teaspoons water to food colouring. Pour liquids into separate parts of rice and fork in to colour it yellow, red and white. Serve hot, garnished with almonds and sultanas.

Serves 4.

Serves 4.

GOLDEN STEAMED CHICKEN

DUCK WITH HONEY & LIME

125 g (4 oz/¾ cup) basmati rice
1.75 kg (3½ lb) chicken
3 tablespoons vegetable oil
½ teaspoon chilli powder
60 g (2 oz/⅓ cup) raisins
60 g (2 oz/½ cup) flaked almonds
1 tablespoon chopped fresh thyme
salt and cayenne pepper
½ teaspoon ground cumin
½ teaspoon turmeric
1 teaspoon ground coriander
2 teaspoons Garam Masala, see page 51
125 ml (4 fl oz/½ cup) hot water
thyme sprigs, to garnish

four 250 g (8 oz) duck portions, skinned
2 tablespoons vegetable oil
1 onion, finely chopped
2 cloves garlic, crushed
2.5 cm (1 in) piece fresh root ginger, finely sliced
8 green cardamom pods, bruised
7.5 cm (3 in) cinnamon stick
3 tablespoons clear honey
juice of 2 limes
twists of lime, to garnish

Wash duck and pat dry with absorbent
kitchen paper. Slash the meaty parts of the
duck 2 or 3 times.

Wash rice thoroughly and soak in cold
water for 30 minutes, then drain. Wash
chicken, pat dry with absorbent kitchen
paper and set aside. Heat 1 tablespoon oil in
a saucepan, add rice and fry, stirring, for 2-3
minutes, until golden brown. Stir in chilli
powder, raisins, almonds, thyme, 185 ml (6
fl oz/¾ cup) water and salt. Bring to the
boil, then cover and simmer for 10-12
minutes, until rice has absorbed all the
liquid. Leave to cool, then use to stuff
chicken.

Place duck in a shallow non-metal dish and
set aside. Heat oil in a frying pan, add onion
and cook, stirring, until soft. Stir in garlic,
ginger, cardamom pods and cinnamon and
fry for 2 minutes more. Stir in honey and
lime juice, then pour over duck portions.
Cover and leave in a cool place for 2-3 hours
to marinate.

Truss chicken, then place in a steamer and
steam for 1 hour. Heat remaining oil in a
large pan, add cumin, turmeric, coriander
and garam masala. Season with salt and
cayenne pepper and fry for 1 minute.
Transfer chicken to this pan and fry for 5
minutes, turning chicken until well coated.
Pour hot water down side of pan, cover and
cook over a low heat for 15-20 minutes,
until tender. Serve hot, garnished with
thyme sprigs.

Preheat oven to 200C (400F/Gas 6). Transfer duck to a roasting tin if shallow dish is
not ovenproof, then cook for 45-60 minutes,
basting occasionally with marinade, until
browned and tender. Serve hot, garnished
with lime twists.

Serves 4.

Serves 4.

MURGHAL SHREDDED DUCK

CHICKEN WITH LENTILS

500 g (1 lb) boneless duck breasts, skinned
60 ml (2 fl oz/¼ cup) vegetable oil
1 onion, finely chopped
1 quantity Cashew Nut Masala made with 125 g (4 oz/
    ¾ cup) cashew nuts, see page 51
1 teaspoon turmeric
60 g (2 oz/⅔ cup) desiccated coconut
90 g (3 oz/½ cup) sultanas
155 ml (5 fl oz/⅔ cup) natural yogurt
6 tablespoons double (thick) cream
60 g (2 oz/⅓ cup) unsalted cashew nuts
1 green chilli, seeded and chopped

Wash duck breasts and pat dry with absorbent kitchen paper.

Slice duck into 0.5 cm (¼ in) thick strips. Heat 3 tablespoons oil in a large frying pan, add duck and cook over a high heat for about 5 minutes, until browned all over. Remove duck from pan with a slotted spoon and set aside. Add onion to pan and cook, stirring, for 5 minutes or until soft. Stir in cashew nut masala and turmeric and fry for 2 minutes. Stir in coconut, sultanas, yogurt, cream and duck.

Cover and cook over a low heat for 15-20 minutes, stirring occasionally, until duck is tender. Just before serving, heat remaining oil in a small pan, add cashew nuts and fry for 2-3 minutes, until golden. Add chilli and fry for 1 minute more. Transfer duck to a warm serving dish, spoon over cashew nut and chilli mixture. Serve hot.

Serves 4-6.

250 g (8 oz) boneless chicken breasts (fillets)
250 g (8 oz/1¼ cups) red split lentils
½ teaspoon turmeric
60 ml (2 fl oz/¼ cup) vegetable oil
6 green cardamom pods, bruised
1 onion, finely sliced
1 cm (½ in) piece fresh root ginger, grated
salt and cayenne pepper
6 teaspoons lemon juice
1 teaspoon cumin seeds
2 cloves garlic, finely sliced

Wash chicken, pat dry and cut into cubes. Set aside.

Wash lentils, put in a large saucepan and add 940 ml (30 fl oz/3¾ cups) water and turmeric. Bring to the boil, then cover and simmer for 20-30 minutes or until tender. Drain thoroughly. Meanwhile, heat half the oil in a large saucepan, add cardamom pods and fry for 1 minute. Add onion and fry, stirring frequently, for about 8 minutes, until golden brown. Add chicken and fry for 5 minutes, until browned all over. Add ginger and fry for 1 minute more. Season with salt and cayenne pepper.

Stir in lemon juice and 155 ml (5 fl oz/⅔ cup) water and cover. Simmer for 25-30 minutes or until chicken is tender. Stir in lentil mixture and cook, stirring, for 5 minutes. Meanwhile, heat remaining oil, add cumin and garlic and fry, stirring, for 1-2 minutes, until garlic is golden. Transfer chicken and lentils to serving dish and pour garlic mixture over. Serve hot.

Serves 4.

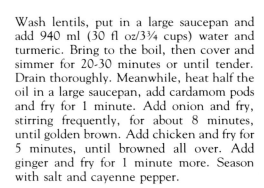

CHICKEN IN SPICY SAUCE

8 chicken thighs, skinned
250 g (8 oz) can tomatoes, drained
6 teaspoons tomato purée (paste)
6 teaspoons chilli sauce
2 teaspoons sugar
3 teaspoons Garam Masala, see page 51
6 teaspoons light soy sauce
5 cm (2 in) piece fresh root ginger, grated
2 cloves garlic, crushed
juice of 1 lime and 1 lemon
twists of lime and lemon, to garnish

Wash chicken and pat dry with absorbent kitchen paper. Slash meaty parts 2 or 3 times. Place in a shallow non-metal dish.

Put tomatoes, tomato purée (paste), chilli sauce, sugar, garam masala, soy sauce, ginger, garlic, and lime and lemon juices in a blender or food processor fitted with a metal blade and process until smooth. Pour over chicken, cover and leave in a cool place for 2-3 hours to allow chicken to absorb flavours.

Preheat oven to 190C (375F/Gas 5). Put chicken and the sauce in a roasting tin and cook, uncovered, for 45-50 minutes, basting with sauce 2 or 3 times, until tender and cooked. Serve hot, garnished with lime and lemon twists.

Serves 4.

CURRIED CHICKEN LIVERS

250 g (8 oz) chicken livers
2 tablespoons vegetable oil
2 onions, finely sliced
3 cloves garlic, crushed
2 teaspoons Garam Masala, see page 51
½ teaspoon turmeric
salt and pepper
6 teaspoons lemon juice
2 tablespoons chopped fresh parsley
parsley sprigs, to garnish

Wash chicken livers and remove any green tinged parts. Set aside.

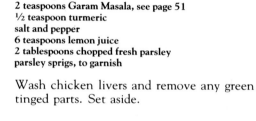

Heat oil in a frying pan, add onions and cook over a medium heat, stirring, for about 8 minutes, until soft and golden brown. Stir in garlic, garam masala and turmeric and season with salt and pepper.

Fry for 1 minute, then stir in chicken livers and fry for about 5 minutes, stirring frequently, until livers are browned on outsides but still slightly pink in the centres. Sprinkle with lemon juice and parsley. Serve hot, garnished with sprigs of parsley.

Serves 4 as a starter.

Note: Frozen chicken livers can be used: thaw at room temperature for 3-4 hours before using.

SWEET SAFFRON RICE

250 g (8 oz/1½ cups) basmati rice
1 teaspoon saffron threads
3 tablespoons boiling water
3 tablespoons vegetable oil
6 cloves
6 green cardamom pods, bruised
7.5 cm (3 in) cinnamon stick
90 g (3 oz/½ cup) raisins
3 tablespoons sugar
salt
parsley sprigs, to garnish

Place rice in a sieve and wash under cold running water until water runs clear.

Put rice in a bowl with 625 ml (20 fl oz/2½ cups) water and soak for 30 minutes. Put saffron in a small bowl, add boiling water and leave to soak for 5 minutes. Heat oil in a heavy-based saucepan, add cloves, cardamom pods and cinnamon and fry for 1 minute. Drain rice and reserve the soaking water. Add rice to the pan and fry for 2-3 minutes, until opaque and light golden.

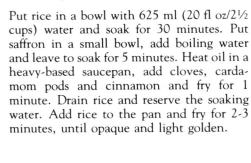

Stir in reserved water, saffron and its soaking water, raisins and sugar and season with salt. Bring to the boil, then lower the heat and simmer, covered, for 12-15 minutes, stirring once or twice, until liquid is absorbed and rice is very tender. Serve hot, garnished with parsley.

Serves 4.

Note: The whole spices in the rice are not meant to be eaten.

FRAGRANT FRIED RICE

185 g (6 oz/1¼ cups) basmati rice
3 tablespoons vegetable oil
8 cloves
4 black cardamom pods, bruised
1 bay leaf
7.5 cm (3 in) cinnamon stick
1 teaspoon black peppercorns
1 teaspoon cumin seeds
1 teaspoon coriander seeds
1 onion, sliced into rings
1 small cauliflower, cut into tiny flowerets
salt
onion rings and bay leaves, to garnish

Place rice in a sieve and wash under cold running water until water runs clear. Put in a bowl with 625 ml (20 fl oz/2½ cups) water and soak for 30 minutes. Heat oil in a heavy-based saucepan, add cloves, cardamom pods, bay leaf, cinnamon, peppercorns and cumin and coriander seeds and fry for 1 minute. Add onion and cook for 5 minutes, until softened. Drain rice and reserve the soaking water.

Add rice to the pan and fry for 2-3 minutes, until opaque and light golden. Stir in reserved water and cauliflower and season with salt. Bring to the boil, lower heat and simmer, covered, for 12-15 minutes, stirring once or twice, until liquid is absorbed and rice and cauliflower are tender. Serve hot, garnished with onion rings and bay leaves.

Serves 4.

Note: Do not eat the whole spices.

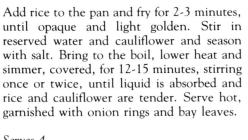

LENTIL-STUFFED PEPPERS

STUFFED OKRA

125 g (4 oz/⅔ cup) red split lentils
60 ml (2 fl oz/¼ cup) vegetable oil
4 green or red peppers (capsicums)
1 teaspoon cumin seeds
2 onions, finely chopped
2 green chillies, seeded and chopped
2.5 cm (1 in) piece fresh root ginger, grated
3 teaspoons ground coriander
salt and pepper
2 tablespoons chopped fresh coriander
coriander leaves, to garnish

Wash lentils, then soak in cold water for 30 minutes.

500 g (1 lb) small okra
6 teaspoons mango powder
3 teaspoons ground coriander
2 teaspoons ground cumin
¼ teaspoon cayenne pepper
1 teaspoon Garam Masala, see page 51
salt
2 tablespoons vegetable oil
1 onion, sliced
6 tomatoes, skinned
lemon slices, to garnish

Wash okra and pat dry with absorbent kitchen paper.

Heat half the oil in a frying pan and fry peppers (capsicums) for 3-5 minutes, until golden brown on all sides. Drain on absorbent kitchen paper and leave to cool. Add remaining oil to pan, then add cumin seeds and fry until just beginning to pop. Add onions and chillies and fry, stirring, for 8 minutes, until onions are soft and golden brown. Stir in ginger and ground coriander. Drain lentils and add to pan with 315 ml (10 fl oz/1¼ cups) water and stir well.

Trim off okra stems, then cut a slit along one side of each pod, stopping 0.5 cm (¼ in) from each end. Mix mango powder, coriander, cumin, cayenne pepper, garam masala and salt to taste together. Prise open okra pods with your thumb and sprinkle a little of the spice mixture inside each pod. Set aside.

Cook, covered, over low heat for 15-20 minutes, until tender and liquid has been absorbed. Season with salt and pepper and add fresh coriander. Preheat oven to 180C (350F/Gas 4). Cut tops from peppers (capsicums) and remove seeds. Stuff peppers (capsicums) with lentil mixture and replace tops. Stand in an ovenproof dish and cook for 15-20 minutes, until soft. Serve hot, garnished with coriander leaves.

Serves 4.

Heat oil in a large saucepan and add onion. Fry for about 5 minutes, until softened. Cut tomatoes into wedges and remove seeds and discard. Add tomatoes to pan and cook, stirring once or twice, for 2 minutes. Add okra and cook gently, covered, for 10-15 minutes, stirring occasionally, until okra are tender. Serve hot, garnished with lemon.

Serves 4.

Note: Mango powder, often called amchoor powder, is available from Asian shops.

DHAL BALLS WITH YOGURT

CARROTS WITH FRESH DILL

125 g (4 oz/⅔ cup) whole green lentils
440 ml (14 fl oz/1¾ cups) natural yogurt
6 tablespoons chopped fresh coriander
¼ teaspoon chilli powder
4 tablespoons shredded fresh coconut
60 g (2 oz/1 cup) fresh breadcrumbs
2 fresh green chillies, seeded and chopped
2.5 cm (1 in) piece fresh root ginger, grated
1 egg, beaten
salt and pepper
60 g (2 oz/½ cup) wholewheat flour
vegetable oil for deep frying
coriander leaves, to garnish

Put lentils in a sieve and wash thoroughly.

500 g (1 lb) carrots
1 tablespoon vegetable oil
30 g (1 oz/6 teaspoons) butter or ghee
¾ teaspoon cumin seeds
pinch ground asafoetida
1 cm (½ in) piece fresh root ginger, finely chopped
2 fresh green chillies, seeded and finely sliced
1 teaspoon ground coriander
¼ teaspoon turmeric
4 tablespoons chopped fresh dill
salt
dill sprigs, to garnish

Cut carrots into 0.3 x 2.5 cm (⅛ x 1 in) sticks and set aside.

Pick over lentils and remove any grit. Put in a bowl, cover with cold water and soak for 2 hours. Meanwhile, mix yogurt with 2 tablespoons coriander, and chilli powder. Cover and chill. Drain lentils, cover with fresh water and simmer for 30 minutes or until tender. Purée in a blender or food processor or mash well. Transfer to a bowl, add 2 tablespoons coconut, breadcrumbs, remaining coriander, chillies, ginger and egg. Season with salt and pepper and mix well. Chill for 30 minutes.

Heat oil and butter or ghee in a heavy-based pan and fry cumin seeds for about 30 seconds, until they begin to pop. Add asafoetida, ginger, chillies, coriander and turmeric and fry for 2 minutes. Stir in carrots and 6 tablespoons water.

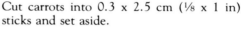
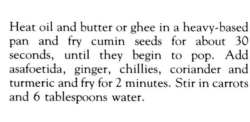

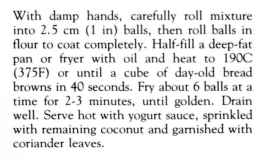

With damp hands, carefully roll mixture into 2.5 cm (1 in) balls, then roll balls in flour to coat completely. Half-fill a deep-fat pan or fryer with oil and heat to 190C (375F) or until a cube of day-old bread browns in 40 seconds. Fry about 6 balls at a time for 2-3 minutes, until golden. Drain well. Serve hot with yogurt sauce, sprinkled with remaining coconut and garnished with coriander leaves.

Serves 4.

Cook over a medium heat, covered, for 5 minutes or until carrots are just tender. Uncover, add chopped dill, season with salt and cook over a high heat for about 2 minutes to evaporate any excess liquid. Serve hot, garnished with dill sprigs.

Serves 4.

Note: This recipe is also delicious, chilled and served as a salad.

MIXED VEGETABLE CURRY

SPICED BROWN LENTILS

3 tablespoons vegetable oil
1 onion, sliced
1 teaspoon ground cumin
1 teaspoon chilli powder
2 teaspoons ground coriander
1 teaspoon turmeric
250 g (8 oz) potatoes, diced
185 g (6 oz) cauliflower flowerets
125 g (4 oz) green beans, sliced
185 g (6 oz) carrots, diced
4 tomatoes, skinned and chopped
315 ml (10 fl oz/1¼ cups) hot vegetable stock
onion rings, to garnish

250 g (8 oz/1¼ cups) whole brown lentils
315 ml (10 fl oz/ 1¼ cups) Coconut Milk, see page 51
¼ teaspoon chilli powder
½ teaspoon turmeric
2 tablespoons vegetable oil
1 onion, finely chopped
4 curry leaves
½ stick lemon grass
7.5 cm (3 in) cinnamon stick
sprigs of lemon thyme, to garnish

Wash lentils, put in a bowl, cover with cold water and leave to soak for 6 hours or overnight.

Heat oil in a large saucepan, add onion and fry for 5 minutes, until softened. Stir in cumin, chilli powder, coriander and turmeric and cook for 2 minutes, stirring occasionally. Add potatoes, cauliflower, green beans and carrots, tossing them in the spices until coated.

Drain lentils and put them in a large saucepan with coconut milk, chilli powder and turmeric. Bring to the boil, then simmer, covered, for 30 minutes or until just tender. Heat oil in a separate pan, add onion, curry leaves, lemon grass and cinnamon and fry over a medium heat, stirring, for 8 minutes or until onion is soft and golden brown.

Add tomatoes and stock and cover. Bring to the boil, then reduce heat and simmer for 10-12 minutes or until vegetables are just tender. Serve hot, garnished with onion rings.

Stir into lentil mixture and simmer for a further 10 minutes or until liquid has evaporated and lentils are soft but not broken up. Remove whole spices and serve hot, garnished with thyme sprigs.

Serves 4.

Serves 4.

Variation: Use any mixture of vegetables to make a total of 750 g (1½ lb) – turnips, swedes, courgettes (zucchini), aubergines (eggplant), parsnips and leeks are all suitable for this curry.

Note: Substitute a few sprigs of lemon thyme if lemon grass is unavailable. Look for lemon grass at Asian and Oriental shops and the larger supermarkets.

CURRIED CHICK-PEAS

TAMIL NADU VEGETABLES

185 g (6 oz/1 cup) dried chick-peas
2 tablespoons vegetable oil
1 small onion, finely chopped
2.5 cm (1 in) piece fresh root ginger, grated
2 cloves garlic, crushed
½ teaspoon turmeric
1 teaspoon ground cumin
1 teaspoon Garam Masala, see page 51
½ teaspoon chilli powder
salt
2 tablespoons chopped fresh coriander

Wash chick-peas well, then put them in a bowl, cover with cold water and leave to soak overnight.

Drain chick-peas, then put in a saucepan with 500 ml (16 fl oz/2 cups) fresh cold water. Bring to the boil for 10 minutes, then reduce heat and simmer, partially covered, for 1 hour. In a separate pan, heat oil, add onion and fry for about 8 minutes, until soft and golden brown.

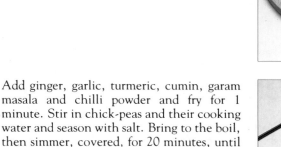

Add ginger, garlic, turmeric, cumin, garam masala and chilli powder and fry for 1 minute. Stir in chick-peas and their cooking water and season with salt. Bring to the boil, then simmer, covered, for 20 minutes, until chick-peas are very tender but still whole. Serve hot, sprinkled with chopped fresh coriander.

Serves 4.

125 g (4 oz/⅔ cup) red split lentils
½ teaspoon turmeric
1 small aubergine (eggplant)
60 ml (2 fl oz/¼ cup) vegetable oil
30 g (1 oz/⅓ cup) desiccated coconut
1 teaspoon cumin seeds
½ teaspoon mustard seeds
2 dried red chillies, crushed
1 red pepper (capsicum), seeded and sliced
125 g (4 oz) courgettes (zucchini), thickly sliced
90 g (3 oz) green beans, cut into 2 cm (¾ in) pieces
155 ml (5 fl oz/⅔ cup) vegetable stock
salt
red pepper (capsicum) strips, to garnish

Wash lentils and put in a large saucepan with turmeric and 625 ml (20 fl oz/2½ cups) water. Bring to the boil, then reduce heat and simmer, covered, for 15-20 minutes, until lentils are soft. Meanwhile, cut aubergine (eggplant) into 1 cm (½ in) dice. Heat oil in a large shallow pan, add coconut, cumin and mustard seeds and chillies.

Fry for 1 minute, then add aubergine (eggplant), red pepper (capsicum), courgettes (zucchini), green beans, stock and salt. Bring to the boil, then simmer, covered, for 10-15 minutes, until the vegetables are just tender. Stir in lentils and any cooking liquid and cook for a further 5 minutes. Serve hot, garnished with red pepper (capsicum) strips.

Serves 4.

MUSHROOM CURRY

500 g (1 lb) button mushrooms
2 fresh green chillies, seeded
2 teaspoons ground coriander
1 teaspoon ground cumin
½ teaspoon chilli powder
2 cloves garlic, crushed
1 onion, cut into wedges
155 ml (5 fl oz/⅔ cup) Coconut Milk, see page 51
salt
30 g (1 oz/6 teaspoons) butter or ghee
bay leaves, to garnish

Wipe mushrooms and trim stalks, then set aside.

Put chillies, ground coriander, cumin, chilli powder, garlic, onion, coconut milk and salt to taste in a blender or food processor fitted with a metal blade and blend until smooth.

Melt butter in a saucepan, add mushrooms and fry for 3-4 minutes, until golden brown. Pour over spicy coconut milk and simmer, uncovered, for 10 minutes or until mushrooms are tender. Serve hot, garnished with bay leaves.

Serves 4.

SPINACH & BEAN DUMPLINGS

185 g (6 oz/1 cup) yellow split mung beans
60 g (2 oz) frozen chopped spinach, thawed
2 tablespoons chopped fresh coriander
2 fresh green chillies, seeded and chopped
large pinch baking powder
½ teaspoon salt
vegetable oil for deep frying
chilli flowers, to garnish

Put beans in a bowl, cover them with water and leave to soak for 4 hours. Drain and rinse under cold running water.

Put beans in a blender or food processor fitted with a metal blade and process until smooth, light and fluffy, scraping mixture from sides of bowl several times. Press excess water from spinach and mix into the ground beans. Stir in coriander, chillies, baking powder and salt.

Half-fill a deep-fat pan or fryer with oil and heat to 190C (375F) or until a cube of day-old bread browns in 40 seconds. Drop 6 heaped teaspoonfuls of mixture into the hot oil and fry for 4-5 minutes or until golden brown. Drain dumplings on absorbent kitchen paper and keep warm while frying remainder. Serve hot, garnished with chilli flowers.

Serves 4.

CHEESY STUFFED TOMATOES

ONION BHAJIS

8 tomatoes
2 tablespoons vegetable oil
1 small onion, finely chopped
1 clove garlic, crushed
2.5 cm (1 in) piece fresh root ginger, grated
1 teaspoon ground cumin
½ teaspoon turmeric
½ teaspoon cayenne pepper
2 teaspoons ground coriander
salt
125 g (4 oz/½ cup) fresh Indian cheese or natural
    fromage frais
30 g (1 oz/¼ cup) Cheddar cheese, grated
1 tablespoon chopped fresh coriander

90 g (3 oz/¾ cup) chick-pea flour, sifted
1 tablespoon vegetable oil plus extra for deep frying
1 teaspoon ground coriander
1 teaspoon ground cumin
2 fresh green chillies, seeded and finely chopped
125 ml (4 fl oz/½ cup) warm water
salt
2 onions, finely sliced
herb sprigs, to garnish

Put flour in blender or food processor fitted
with a metal blade.

Cut a slice from the top of each tomato.
Scoop out centres and discard seeds, then
chop pulp and reserve. Turn tomatoes
upside down on absorbent kitchen paper and
leave to drain. Heat oil in a small frying pan,
add onion and fry for 5 minutes, stirring
occasionally, until soft. Stir in garlic and
ginger and fry for 1 minute. Stir in cumin,
turmeric, cayenne pepper and ground
coriander. Season with salt and fry for 1
minute more.

Add oil, coriander, cumin, chillies and
water. Season with salt. Process until well
blended and smooth, then pour batter into a
bowl. Cover and leave in a warm place for
30 minutes. Stir in onions.

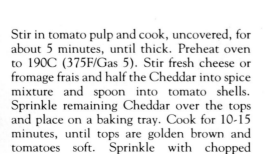

Stir in tomato pulp and cook, uncovered, for
about 5 minutes, until thick. Preheat oven
to 190C (375F/Gas 5). Stir fresh cheese or
fromage frais and half the Cheddar into spice
mixture and spoon into tomato shells.
Sprinkle remaining Cheddar over the tops
and place on a baking tray. Cook for 10-15
minutes, until tops are golden brown and
tomatoes soft. Sprinkle with chopped
coriander and serve hot.

Serves 4.

Half-fill a deep-fat pan or fryer with oil and
heat to 190C (375F) or until a cube of day-
old bread browns in 40 seconds. Drop about
five 2 tablespoon amounts into the oil and
fry for 5-6 minutes, until golden. Drain on
absorbent kitchen paper. Serve hot, garnished with sprigs of herbs.

Serves 4.

Note: Make sure that the oil doesn't become
too hot: the bhajis must fry slowly so the
centres cook through.

SPICY OKRA

375 g (12 oz) okra
2 tablespoons vegetable oil
2.5 cm (1 in) piece fresh root ginger, grated
1 teaspoon turmeric
½ teaspoon chilli powder
1 teaspoon chick-pea flour
salt
315 ml (10 fl oz/1¼ cups) natural yogurt
2 tablespoons chopped fresh coriander, to garnish

Wash okra and pat dry with absorbent kitchen paper, then cut into thick slices.

Heat oil in a saucepan, add okra and fry, stirring occasionally, for 4 minutes. Stir in ginger, turmeric, chilli powder and flour. Season with salt and fry for 1 minute more.

Stir in 3 tablespoons water, then cover and cook gently for 10 minutes or until okra is tender. Stir in yogurt and reheat gently. Serve hot, sprinkled with coriander.

Serves 4.

Note: Choose okra pods that are about 10 cm (4 in) long – larger pods are tough and stringy to eat.

DRY POTATO CURRY

500 g (1 lb) waxy potatoes
salt
2 tablespoons vegetable oil
1 teaspoon mustard seeds
1 onion, finely sliced
2 cloves garlic, crushed
2.5 cm (1 in) piece fresh root ginger, grated
1 fresh green chilli, seeded and chopped
1 teaspoon turmeric
½ teaspoon cayenne pepper
1 teaspoon ground cumin
green pepper (capsicum) strips, to garnish, if desired

Cut potatoes into 2 cm (¾ in) chunks.

Cook potatoes in boiling salted water for 6-8 minutes, until just tender, then drain and set aside. Heat oil in a large saucepan, add mustard seeds and fry for 30 seconds or until they begin to pop. Add onion and fry for 5 minutes, until soft but not brown. Stir in garlic and ginger and fry for 1 minute more.

Add potatoes, chilli, turmeric, cayenne and cumin and stir well. Cook, covered, for 3-5 minutes, stirring occasionally, until potatoes are very tender and coated with spices. Serve hot, garnished with green pepper (capsicum) strips, if desired.

Serves 4.

FISH IN A PACKET

HOT MUSSELS WITH CUMIN

four 185-250 g (6-8 oz) fish steaks, such as sea bass, cod or salmon
1-2 fresh or frozen banana leaves, optional
salt and pepper
60 g (2 oz/1¼ cups) finely grated fresh coconut
60 g (2 oz) fresh mint, chopped
4 cloves garlic, crushed
1 teaspoon ground cumin
4 fresh green chillies, seeded and chopped
6 teaspoons lemon juice
60 ml (2 fl oz/¼ cup) cider vinegar
1 tablespoon vegetable oil
8 dried curry leaves, optional
mint leaves and lemon slices, to garnish

1.5 kg (3 lb) mussels
2 tablespoons vegetable oil
1 large onion, finely chopped
2.5 cm (1 in) piece fresh root ginger, grated
6 cloves garlic, crushed
2 fresh green chillies, seeded and finely chopped
½ teaspoon turmeric
2 teaspoons ground cumin
90 g (3 oz/1¾ cups) shredded fresh coconut
2 tablespoons chopped fresh coriander
coriander sprigs, to garnish

Scrub mussels clean in several changes of fresh cold water and pull off beards.

Wipe fish steaks and place each in centre of a 30 cm (12 in) square of banana leaf, if using, or foil. Sprinkle fish with salt and pepper. Mix together coconut, mint, garlic, cumin, chillies and lemon juice. Spoon a quarter of mixture over each fish steak. Fold sides of banana leaf or foil over to seal completely. Tie banana leaf parcels with fine string, if necessary.

Discard any mussels that are cracked or do not close tightly when tapped. Set aside. Heat oil in a large saucepan and add onion. Fry, stirring, for 5 minutes, until soft, then add ginger, garlic, chillies, turmeric and cumin. Fry 2 minutes, stirring constantly.

Pour vinegar, oil and 185 ml (6 fl oz/¾ cup) water into base of a large steamer, add curry leaves and bring to the boil. Steam parcels for 12-15 minutes or until fish flakes easily. Open parcels and serve, garnished with mint and lemon slices.

Serves 4.

Add mussels, coconut and 250 ml (8 fl oz/1 cup) water and bring to the boil. Cover and cook over a high heat, shaking pan frequently, for about 5 minutes or until almost all the shells have opened. Discard any that do not open. Spoon mussels into a serving dish, pour over cooking liquid and sprinkle with chopped coriander. Garnish with coriander sprigs and serve at once.

Serves 4.

CORIANDER & CHILLI FISH

SOLE WITH DILL STUFFING

875 g (1¾ lb) white fish fillets, such as monkfish,
  sole or plaice
4 teaspoons lemon juice
salt and pepper
90 g (3 oz) fresh coriander leaves
4 fresh green chillies, seeded and chopped
3 cloves garlic, crushed
250 ml (8 fl oz/1 cup) natural yogurt
vegetable oil for deep frying
lemon wedges and coriander leaves, to garnish

Trim any skin and bones from fish, then cut
flesh into 2.5 x 7.5 cm (1 x 3 in) strips.

four 185 g (6 oz) sole fillets, skinned
3 teaspoons lemon juice
salt and pepper
2 tablespoons vegetable oil
1 clove garlic, crushed
2.5 cm (1 in) piece fresh root ginger, grated
¼ teaspoon cayenne pepper
¼ teaspoon turmeric
4 spring onions, finely chopped
8 tablespoons finely chopped fresh dill
dill sprigs, to garnish

Wash fish fillets and pat dry with absorbent
kitchen paper.

Spread fish strips in a shallow non-metal
dish and sprinkle with lemon juice and salt
and pepper. Set aside in a cool place. Put
coriander, chillies, garlic and 1-2 tablespoons water in a blender or food processor
fitted with a metal blade and process until
smooth, frequently scraping mixture down
from sides. Squeeze out excess liquid from
paste, place in a shallow dish and stir in
yogurt.

Lay fillets skinned-side up on a work surface
and sprinkle with lemon juice and salt and
pepper, then set aside. Preheat oven to
180C (350F/Gas 4). Heat 1½ tablespoons
oil in a frying pan. Add garlic, ginger,
cayenne, turmeric and spring onions and
cook over a low heat for 3 minutes or until
onions are soft and golden, stirring occasionally. Remove from heat and set aside to
cool, then stir in dill.

Heat oil in a deep-fat pan or fryer to 180C
(350F) or until a cube of day-old bread
browns in 35 seconds. Drain fish and pat dry
with absorbent kitchen paper. Dip the strips
in yogurt mixture, coating them all over and
fry a few at a time for 2-3 minutes, until
golden brown. Drain on absorbent kitchen
paper, then serve at once, garnished with
lemon wedges and coriander leaves.

Serves 4.

Divide stuffing between fillets and spread
evenly over skinned side of fish. Roll fillets
up from thickest end. Grease a shallow
ovenproof dish with remaining oil and
arrange sole rolls, seam-side down, in the
dish with 60 ml (2 fl oz/¼ cup) water. Cover
with foil and cook for 15-20 minutes or until
fish flakes easily. Serve hot, with cooking
juices spooned over and garnished with
sprigs of dill.

Serves 4.

SPICE & GARLIC FISH FRY

750 g (1½ lb) mixed white fish fillets, such as sole, plaice, whiting, cod or monkfish
1 teaspoon ground cumin
½ teaspoon ground coriander
1 teaspoon ground aniseed
½ teaspoon chilli powder
3 cloves garlic, crushed
3 teaspoons lemon juice
salt
vegetable oil for deep frying
lettuce leaves and lemon slices, to garnish

Remove any skin and bones from fish, wash and pat dry with absorbent kitchen paper. Cut into large chunks.

Mix cumin, coriander, aniseed, chilli powder, garlic, lemon juice and salt together, blending to a smooth paste. Spread over fish, cover and leave in a cool place for 1 hour.

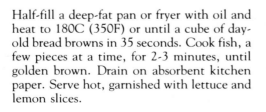

Half-fill a deep-fat pan or fryer with oil and heat to 180C (350F) or until a cube of day-old bread browns in 35 seconds. Cook fish, a few pieces at a time, for 2-3 minutes, until golden brown. Drain on absorbent kitchen paper. Serve hot, garnished with lettuce and lemon slices.

Serves 4.

SPICY PRAWN PATTIES

375 g (12 oz) white fish fillets, such as sole, plaice, cod or whiting
185 g (6 oz) peeled cooked prawns, chopped
4 spring onions, chopped
2.5 cm (1 in) piece fresh root ginger, grated
2 tablespoons chopped fresh coriander
1 tablespoon chopped fresh mint
125 g (4 oz/2 cups) fresh white breadcrumbs
salt and cayenne pepper
1 egg yolk, beaten
6 teaspoons lemon juice
90 g (3 oz/¾ cup) chick-pea flour
3 teaspoons ground coriander
60 ml (2 fl oz/¼ cup) vegetable oil for frying
mint sprigs and lemon slices, to garnish

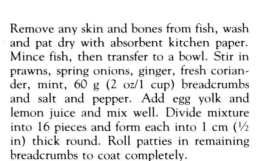

Remove any skin and bones from fish, wash and pat dry with absorbent kitchen paper. Mince fish, then transfer to a bowl. Stir in prawns, spring onions, ginger, fresh coriander, mint, 60 g (2 oz/1 cup) breadcrumbs and salt and pepper. Add egg yolk and lemon juice and mix well. Divide mixture into 16 pieces and form each into 1 cm (½ in) thick round. Roll patties in remaining breadcrumbs to coat completely.

Put flour and ground coriander in a small bowl, season with salt and cayenne pepper, then add 125 ml (4 fl oz/½ cup) water and mix to a smooth batter. Heat oil in a frying pan. Dip prawn patties in batter, then fry for 2-3 minutes on each side until golden brown. Drain on absorbent kitchen paper and serve hot, garnished with mint and lemon slices.

Serves 4.

FISH IN HOT SAUCE

STEAMED FISH & VEGETABLES

four 250 g (8 oz) whole fish, such as mackerel, trout,
   grey mullet or blue fish, cleaned
4 dill sprigs
4 lime slices
60 ml (2 fl oz/¼ cup) vegetable oil
4 spring onions, sliced
1 cm (½ in) piece fresh root ginger, grated
1 clove garlic, crushed
1 teaspoon mustard seeds
¼ teaspoon cayenne pepper
3 teaspoons tamarind paste
6 teaspoons tomato purée (paste)
dill sprigs and lime slices, to garnish

four 250 g (8 oz) whole red mullet, red snapper or sea
   bream, cleaned
4 teaspoons Garam Masala, see page 51
½ teaspoon turmeric
2 tablespoons chopped fresh coriander
1 tablespoon chopped fresh parsley
2.5 cm (1 in) piece fresh root ginger, grated
4 lemon slices
2 tablespoons vegetable oil
8 new potatoes, sliced
3 carrots, sliced
4 courgettes (zucchini), sliced
salt and pepper
coriander leaves, to garnish

Wash fish and pat dry with absorbent
kitchen paper. Slash 2 or 3 times on each
side, tuck a sprig of dill and a lime slice
inside each fish, then set aside. Heat 2
tablespoons of oil in a small pan. Add
onions and cook, stirring, for 2-3 minutes,
until softened. Add ginger, garlic and mustard seeds and fry for 1 minute more, until
mustard seeds start to pop.

Wash fish and pat dry with absorbent
kitchen paper, then slash 3 times on each
side. Mix garam masala, turmeric, coriander, parsley and ginger together and rub into
flesh and skin of fish. Tuck a slice of lemon
inside each fish and set aside. Heat oil in a
frying pan, add potatoes and carrots and fry,
stirring frequently, for 5-6 minutes, until
slightly softened and beginning to brown.

Stir in cayenne pepper, tamarind paste,
tomato purée (paste) and 90 ml (3 fl oz/⅓
cup) water. Bring to the boil and simmer,
uncovered, for about 5 minutes, until thickened slightly. Meanwhile, heat grill. Place
fish on grill rack, brush with remaining oil
and cook for about 5 minutes on each side,
basting occasionally with oil, until flesh
flakes easily. Serve hot with the sauce,
garnished with dill and lime slices.

Serves 4.

Add courgettes (zucchini) to pan and fry for
1 minute more. Season with salt and pepper.
Using a slotted spoon, transfer vegetables to
a steamer. Lay fish on top, cover and steam
for 20-25 minutes or until fish flakes easily
and vegetables are tender. Serve at once,
garnished with coriander.

Serves 4.

PRAWN & FISH BALL CURRY

CREAMY SAFFRON FISH CURRY

500 g (1 lb) white fish fillets, such as sole, plaice, cod,
   whiting or monkfish, skinned
125 g (4 oz) peeled cooked prawns
90 g (3 oz/1½ cups) fresh white breadcrumbs
2 eggs, beaten separately
2 tablespoons chopped fresh coriander
2 teaspoons lemon juice
salt and pepper
2 tablespoons vegetable oil plus extra for frying
1 large onion, finely chopped
2 fresh green chillies, seeded and chopped
4 cloves garlic, crushed
½ teaspoon turmeric
155 ml (5 fl oz/⅔ cup) Coconut Milk, see page 51
440 g (14 oz) can chopped tomatoes

750 g (1½ lb) white fish fillets, such as sole, plaice,
   whiting or cod
pinch saffron threads
2 tablespoons boiling water
3 tablespoons vegetable oil
2 onions, chopped
3 cloves garlic, crushed
2.5 cm (1 in) piece fresh root ginger, grated
1 teaspoon turmeric
3 teaspoons ground coriander
2 teaspoons Garam Masala, see page 51
salt and cayenne pepper
2 teaspoons chick-pea flour
250 ml (8 fl oz/1 cup) natural yogurt
60 ml (2 fl oz/¼ cup) double (thick) cream
lemon peel and red pepper (capsicum), to garnish

Wash fish and remove any bones. Mince fish
and prawns, then transfer to a large bowl.
Stir in 60 g (2 oz/1 cup) breadcrumbs, 1 egg,
coriander and lemon juice and season with
salt and pepper. Mix well and form into 24
balls. Roll balls in remaining egg, then in
remaining breadcrumbs to coat completely.
Chill for 30 minutes. Meanwhile, heat 2
tablespoons oil in a heavy-based pan, add
onion and cook, stirring, for 5 minutes until
soft.

Wash fish, remove any skin and bones and
pat dry with absorbent paper. Cut into large
chunks and set aside. Put saffron in a small
bowl with water and leave to soak for about
5 minutes. Heat oil in a large shallow pan,
add onions and cook, stirring, for about 5
minutes, until soft but not coloured.

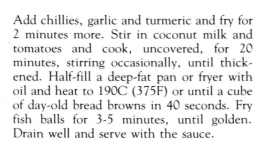

Add chillies, garlic and turmeric and fry for
2 minutes more. Stir in coconut milk and
tomatoes and cook, uncovered, for 20
minutes, stirring occasionally, until thickened. Half-fill a deep-fat pan or fryer with
oil and heat to 190C (375F) or until a cube
of day-old bread browns in 40 seconds. Fry
fish balls for 3-5 minutes, until golden.
Drain well and serve with the sauce.

Serves 4.

Add garlic, ginger, turmeric, coriander,
garam masala and salt and pepper and fry for
1 minute more. Stir in flour and cook for 1
minute, then remove from heat. Stir in
yogurt and cream, then return to heat and
slowly bring to the boil. Add fish, saffron
and soaking water and simmer gently, covered, for 10-15 minutes, until fish is tender
and flakes easily. Serve the fish hot, garnished with shreds of lemon peel and red
pepper (capsicum).

Serves 4.

COCONUT SPICED COD

four 185-250 g (6-8 oz) cod steaks
salt and pepper
2 tablespoons vegetable oil
1 onion, chopped
125 g (4 oz/1⅓ cups) desiccated coconut
5 cm (2 in) piece fresh root ginger, grated
2 cloves garlic, crushed
2 green chillies, seeded and chopped
½ teaspoon chilli powder
grated peel and juice of 1 lemon
2 tablespoons chopped fresh coriander
2 tomatoes, skinned, seeded and diced
oregano leaves, to garnish

Wash cod steaks and pat dry with absorbent kitchen paper. Place in a greased ovenproof dish and sprinkle with salt and pepper. Heat oil in a frying pan, add onion and fry, stirring, for about 5 minutes or until soft. Stir in coconut, ginger, garlic, chillies and chilli powder and fry, stirring, for 3-5 minutes, until golden brown.

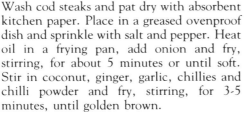

Stir in lemon peel and juice and simmer, covered, for 10 minutes to soften coconut. Preheat oven to 160C (325F/Gas 3). Stir coriander and tomatoes into coconut mixture and spoon over cod steaks. Cook for 20-25 minutes, until fish flakes easily. Serve hot, garnished with oregano leaves.

Serves 4.

Note: Cover with foil during cooking if coconut begins to brown too much.

GRILLED SPICED FISH

four 250 g (8 oz) whole plaice or flounder, skinned
salt and pepper
155 ml (5 fl oz/⅔ cup) natural yogurt
2 cloves garlic, crushed
2 teaspoons Garam Masala, see page 51
1 teaspoon ground coriander
½ teaspoon chilli powder
3 teaspoons lemon juice
lemon wedges and parsley sprigs, to garnish

Wash fish, pat dry with absorbent kitchen paper and place in a shallow non-metal dish. Sprinkle with salt and pepper.

Mix together yogurt, garlic, garam masala, coriander, chilli powder and lemon juice. Pour over fish and cover. Leave in a cool place for 2-3 hours to allow fish to absorb flavours.

Heat grill. Transfer fish to a grill rack and cook for about 8 minutes, basting with cooking juices and turning over halfway through cooking, until fish flakes easily. Serve hot, garnished with lemon wedges and parsley sprigs.

Serves 4.

Note: Use fillets instead of whole fish, if preferred, and grill for about 2 minutes less.

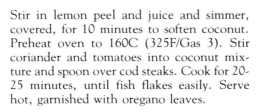

CARROT HALVA

PISTACHIO HALVA

625 g (1¼ lb) carrots, coarsely grated
750 ml (24 fl oz/3 cups) milk
8 green cardamom pods, bruised
60 ml (2 fl oz/¼ cup) vegetable oil
60 g (2 oz/¼ cup) caster sugar
30 g (1 oz/2 tablespoons) sultanas
60 g (2 oz/⅓ cup) shelled pistachio nuts, coarsely
    chopped
250 ml (8 fl oz/1 cup) strained Greek yogurt, to serve

Put carrots, milk and cardamom pods in a
heavy-based saucepan and bring to the boil
over a high heat.

185 g (6 oz/1¼ cups) shelled pistachio nuts
250 ml (8 fl oz/1 cup) boiling water
2 tablespoons milk
125 g (4 oz/½ cup) sugar
22 g (¾ oz/4½ teaspoons) butter or ghee
few drops vanilla essence

Put pistachio nuts in a bowl, pour over
boiling water and leave to soak for 30
minutes. Grease and base-line an 18 cm (7
in) square tin.

Reduce the heat to medium and cook,
uncovered, for about 50 minutes, stirring
occasionally, until liquid has been absorbed.
Heat oil in a large frying pan, add carrot
mixture and fry, stirring constantly, for
10-15 minutes, until mixture turns a deep
red colour.

Drain pistachio nuts thoroughly and put in a
blender or food processor fitted with a metal
blade. Add milk and process until finely
chopped, scraping mixture down from sides
once or twice. Stir in sugar. Heat a large
non-stick frying pan, add butter or ghee and
melt over a low to medium heat. Add nut
paste and cook for about 15 minutes, stirring
constantly, until mixture is very thick.

Stir in sugar, sultanas and half the pistachios. Cook for 1-2 minutes more to heat
through. Serve warm, topped with yogurt
and sprinkled with remaining pistachio nuts.

Serves 6-8.

Stir in vanilla essence, then spoon into
prepared tin and spread evenly. Leave to
cool completely, then cut into 20 squares
using a sharp knife.

Makes about 20 squares.

Note: This halva will keep for 2-3 weeks,
stored in the refrigerator.

SAFFRON YOGURT

CARDAMOM & NUT ICE CREAM

625 ml (20 fl oz/2½ cups) natural yogurt
pinch saffron threads
6 teaspoons boiling water
seeds from 6 cardamom pods
9 teaspoons caster sugar
lemon peel and cardamom seeds, to decorate

Pour yogurt into a nylon sieve lined with muslin and leave in refrigerator overnight to drain.

Put saffron and water in a small bowl and leave to soak for 30 minutes. Tip drained yogurt into a bowl and stir in saffron and its soaking liquid.

Put cardamom seeds in a mortar and crush lightly with a pestle. Stir into yogurt with sugar. Serve chilled, decorated with lemon peel and cardamom seeds.

Serves 4-6.

2 litres (3½ pints/8 cups) milk
12 green cardamom pods, bruised
90 g (3 oz/⅓ cup) caster sugar
45 g (1½ oz/⅓ cup) chopped blanched almonds, toasted
45 g (1½ oz/⅓ cup) chopped pistachio nuts
mint sprigs, to decorate

Put milk and cardamom pods in a large heavy-based pan and bring to the boil. Reduce heat to medium-low and simmer, uncovered, stirring frequently, for 30 minutes or until milk is reduced by about two-thirds. Remove cardamom pods with a slotted spoon and discard.

Stir in sugar, almonds and half the pistachio nuts and simmer for 5 minutes more. Leave to cool. Pour reduced milk into a plastic container, cover and freeze for 2-3 hours, until frozen around edge. Spoon into a food processor fitted with a metal blade and process until smooth and light. Return to container, cover and freeze for 1 hour. Meanwhile, put 6 individual 185 ml (6 fl oz/¾ cup) moulds into freezer to chill.

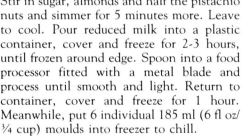

Spoon semi-frozen mixture into moulds, pressing down firmly. Cover and freeze for 2-3 hours, until solid. To serve, dip moulds in hot water for a few seconds and turn out onto plates. Serve at once, sprinkled with remaining pistachio nuts and decorated with mint sprigs.

Serves 6.

Note: If preferred, whisk ice cream with an electric whisk instead of a food processor.

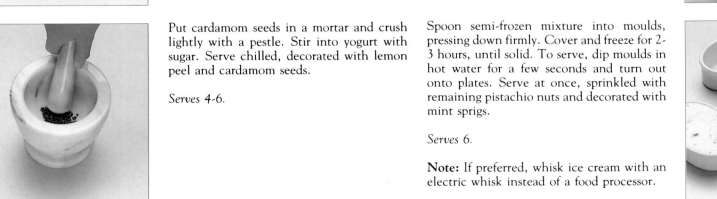

SAFFRON RICE PUDDING

COCONUT PANCAKES

185 g (6 oz/1¼ cups) basmati rice
75 ml (2½ fl oz/⅓ cup) milk
pinch saffron threads
30 g (1 oz/6 teaspoons) butter
2 green cardamom pods, bruised
2.5 cm (1 in) cinnamon stick
2 cloves
90 g (3 oz/½ cup) sultanas
60 g (2 oz/¼ cup) caster sugar
45 g (1½ oz/⅓ cup) flaked almonds, toasted

Wash rice under cold running water and put into a large saucepan with 625 ml (20 fl oz/ 2½ cups) cold water.

Bring to the boil, then reduce heat and simmer, covered, for 5 minutes. Drain. Measure 6 teaspoons milk into a small bowl, add saffron and leave to soak for 5 minutes. Melt butter in a heavy-based saucepan, add rice, cardamom pods, cinnamon and cloves and fry for 2-3 minutes or until rice becomes opaque.

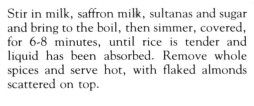

Stir in milk, saffron milk, sultanas and sugar and bring to the boil, then simmer, covered, for 6-8 minutes, until rice is tender and liquid has been absorbed. Remove whole spices and serve hot, with flaked almonds scattered on top.

Serves 4.

125 g (4 oz/1 cup) plain flour
pinch salt
1 egg, beaten
about 315 ml (10 fl oz/1¼ cups) milk
45 g (1½ oz/9 teaspoons) demerara sugar
220 g (7 oz/4 cups) shredded fresh coconut
1 cm (½ in) piece fresh root ginger, grated
6 aniseeds, crushed
natural yogurt, to serve

Sift flour and salt together into a mixing bowl. Whisk in egg and half of the milk to make a smooth, thick batter.

Set batter aside in a cool place for 30 minutes, then stir in enough of remaining milk to make batter the consistency of single (light) cream. Heat a 15 cm (6 in) frying pan, brush with a little oil and pour in 2-3 tablespoons batter, tipping pan to coat base. Cook over a medium to high heat for 1-2 minutes, until browned, then flip pancake over with a palette knife and cook other side for about 30 seconds, until browned.

Turn pancake onto a plate and make 7 more pancakes in same way, stacking them on the plate as they are ready. In a small bowl, mix together sugar, 185 g (6 oz/3⅔ cups) coconut, ginger and aniseed. Spread a spoonful of mixture on each pancake and fold into quarters. Cover and chill for about 30 minutes. Decorate with remaining coconut sprinkled over tops, and serve cold with yogurt.

Serves 4.

GOLDEN SEMOLINA PUDDING

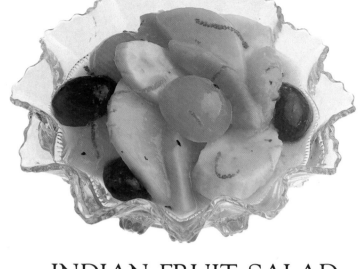

INDIAN FRUIT SALAD

125 g (4 oz/½ cup) caster sugar
45 g (1½ oz/9 teaspoons) butter or ghee
125 g (4 oz/¾ cup) semolina
seeds from 3 cardamom pods
30 g (1 oz/¼ cup) raisins
60 g (2 oz/½ cup) flaked almonds, toasted

Put sugar in a heavy-based saucepan with
155 ml (5 fl oz/⅔ cup) water. Cook over a
low heat, stirring occasionally, until sugar
has dissolved. Bring to the boil and boil for 1
minute, then remove from heat and set
aside.

2 mangoes
2 bananas
2 oranges
60 g (2 oz) black grapes
60 g (2 oz) green grapes
1 papaya (paw paw)
grated peel and juice of 1 lime
60 g (2 oz/¼ cup) caster sugar
freshly ground black pepper
natural yogurt, to serve

Peel and stone mangoes and cut flesh into
thin slices, reserving any scraps. Peel and
diagonally slice bananas.

Melt butter or ghee in a large heavy-based
frying pan, add semolina and cook for 8-10
minutes over a medium heat, stirring constantly, until semolina turns golden brown.

Peel and segment oranges, working over a
bowl to catch juices. Halve and pip both
black and green grapes. Peel and halve
papaya (paw paw), scoop out seeds and cut
flesh into slices, reserving any scraps. Put
fruit in a serving bowl and stir to combine.

Remove from heat and leave to cool slightly,
then stir in sugar syrup and cardamom seeds.
Cook over a low heat for 3-5 minutes,
stirring frequently, until thick. Stir in half
the raisins and almonds. Serve warm, decorated with remaining raisins and almonds.

Serves 4-6.

Note: Serve with natural yogurt, if desired.

Put orange juice, lime juice, sugar and scraps
of mango and papaya (paw paw) in a blender
or food processor fitted with a metal blade
and process until smooth. Add lime peel and
pepper. Pour over fruit and chill for at least 1
hour before serving with yogurt.

Serves 4-6.

Note: Use other fruits, such as melon, guava
or pineapple, if preferred.

TOASTED ALMOND TOFFEE

500 g (1 lb/2 cups) sugar
155 g (5 oz/2 cups) low-fat milk powder
few drops vanilla essence
30 g (1 oz/¼ cup) flaked almonds, toasted

Grease and base-line an 18 cm (7 in) square tin. Put sugar in a large heavy-based saucepan with 250 ml (8 fl oz/1 cup) water and heat gently, stirring occasionally, until sugar is dissolved.

Bring to the boil, then boil over a medium-high heat until a few drops of mixture will form a soft ball in cold water. Stir in milk powder and cook for 3-4 minutes more, stirring constantly, until mixture begins to dry on spoon. Stir in vanilla.

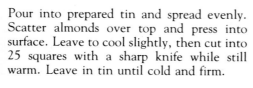

Pour into prepared tin and spread evenly. Scatter almonds over top and press into surface. Leave to cool slightly, then cut into 25 squares with a sharp knife while still warm. Leave in tin until cold and firm.

Makes 25 squares.

COCONUT LAYER CAKE

60 g (2 oz/½ cup) plain flour
440 ml (14 fl oz/1⅔ cups) Coconut Milk, see page 51
6 egg yolks, beaten
125 g (4 oz/½ cup) caster sugar
seeds from 4 green cardamom pods, crushed
pinch freshly grated nutmeg
125 g (4 oz/½ cup) butter, melted
natural yogurt and slices of banana, to serve

Put flour in a mixing bowl, whisk in coconut milk, egg yolks, sugar, cardamom seeds and nutmeg, then leave batter to stand for 30 minutes.

Preheat oven to 220C (425F/Gas 7). Butter and base-line a 15 cm (6 in) soufflé dish. Add 3 teaspoons butter to dish and heat in oven for 5 minutes. Pour in one-seventh (5-6 tablespoons) of batter and bake for 10-15 minutes, until firm to touch and lightly browned. Continue adding another 3 layers, brushing cooked layer with butter before adding batter, then cooking each layer for 10-15 minutes.

Put soufflé dish in a roasting tin half-filled with boiling water, then continue adding final 3 layers in same way as before. When last layer is cooked, remove dish from oven and leave to cool. Run a knife around edge of dish to loosen cake and turn out onto a serving plate. Serve warm, with yogurt and sliced bananas.

Serves 4-6.

APRICOT DESSERT

CASHEW NUT FUDGE

250 g (8 oz/1¾ cups) ready-to-eat dried apricots
250 g (8 oz/1 cup) caster sugar
250 ml (8 fl oz/1 cup) whipping cream
60 g (2 oz/⅓ cup) blanched almonds, chopped and
   toasted

Put apricots in a saucepan with 250 ml (8 fl oz/1 cup) water and bring to the boil, then simmer, covered, for about 25 minutes or until very soft.

250 g (8 oz/1½ cups) unsalted cashew nuts
375 ml (12 fl oz/1½ cups) boiling water
6 teaspoons milk
155 g (5 oz/⅔ cup) sugar
15 g (½ oz/3 teaspoons) butter or ghee
few drops vanilla essence
few sheets silver leaf

Put cashew nuts in a bowl, pour over boiling water and leave to soak for 1 hour. Grease and base-line an 18 cm (7 in) square tin.

Meanwhile, put sugar and 500 ml (16 fl oz/2 cups) water in a heavy-based saucepan and heat gently, stirring occasionally, until sugar has dissolved. Bring to the boil and boil for 3 minutes or until syrupy. Drain apricots and purée in a blender or food processor fitted with a metal blade. Add syrup and process again.

Drain cashew nuts thoroughly and put in a blender or food processor fitted with a metal blade. Add milk and process until smooth, scraping mixture down from sides once or twice. Stir in sugar. Heat a large non-stick frying pan, add butter or ghee and melt over a low to medium heat. Add nut paste and cook for about 20 minutes, stirring constantly, until mixture is very thick.

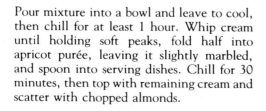

Pour mixture into a bowl and leave to cool, then chill for at least 1 hour. Whip cream until holding soft peaks, fold half into apricot purée, leaving it slightly marbled, and spoon into serving dishes. Chill for 30 minutes, then top with remaining cream and scatter with chopped almonds.

Serves 4-6.

Stir in vanilla essence, then spoon into prepared tin and spread evenly. Leave to cool completely, then press silver leaf onto surface. Cut fudge into about 25 diamond shapes using a wet sharp knife.

Makes about 25 pieces.

Note: This fudge will keep for 2-3 weeks if stored in an airtight tin.

FRESH MANGO CHUTNEY

LIME PICKLE

2 mangoes
1 red chilli, seeded and finely sliced
30 g (1 oz/¼ cup) cashew nuts, chopped
30 g (1 oz/¼ cup) raisins
2 tablespoons chopped fresh mint
pinch asafoetida
½ teaspoon ground cumin
¼ teaspoon cayenne pepper
½ teaspoon ground coriander
mint sprigs, to garnish

Peel and stone mangoes, then very thinly slice flesh.

Put mango slices in a bowl with chilli, cashew nuts, raisins and mint and stir gently. In a small bowl, mix asafoetida, cumin, cayenne and coriander together, then sprinkle over mango mixture.

Stir gently to coat mango mixture in spices, then cover and chill for 2 hours. Serve chilled, garnished with mint sprigs.

Makes about 250 g (8 oz).

12 limes
60 g (2 oz/¼ cup) coarse sea salt
3 teaspoons fenugreek seeds
3 teaspoons mustard seeds
6 teaspoons chilli powder
3 teaspoons ground turmeric
250 ml (8 fl oz/1 cup) vegetable oil, such as sunflower
  or peanut
coriander sprigs, to garnish

Cut each lime lengthwise into 8 thin wedges. Place in a large sterilised bowl, sprinkle with salt and set aside.

Put fenugreek and mustard seeds in a frying pan and dry roast them over a medium heat for 1-2 minutes, until they begin to pop. Put them in a mortar and grind them to a fine powder with a pestle.

Add chilli powder and turmeric and mix well. Sprinkle spice mixture over limes and stir. Pour over oil and cover with a dry cloth. Leave in a sunny place for 10-12 days, until softened. Pack into sterilised jars, then seal and store in a cool, dark place. It can be kept for 1-2 weeks. Serve at room temperature, garnished with coriander.

Makes about 1.5 kg (3 lb).

Variation: To make Lemon Pickle, substitute 8 lemons for the limes.

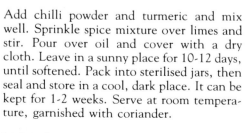

SAUTÉED CHILLI PICKLE

2 teaspoons sesame seeds
1 teaspoon fennel seeds
2 teaspoons coriander seeds
2 teaspoons cumin seeds
60 ml (2 fl oz/¼ cup) vegetable oil
½ teaspoon black peppercorns
20 fresh green chillies
1 teaspoon mango powder
9 teaspoons lemon juice
grated lemon peel, to garnish, if desired

Put sesame, fennel, coriander and cumin seeds in a frying pan. Dry roast over a medium heat until spices begin to pop.

Add oil, peppercorns, chillies and mango powder and fry, stirring, for 3-5 minutes or until chillies are softened. Transfer to a serving dish, sprinkle over lemon juice and leave to cool. Serve at room temperature, garnished with lemon peel, if desired.

Makes about 185 g (6 oz).

Note: For a less hot pickle, halve and seed chillies before frying.

AUBERGINE PICKLE

750 g (1½ lb) baby aubergines (eggplants)
½ teaspoon turmeric
salt
500 ml (16 fl oz/2 cups) vegetable oil
6 cloves garlic, crushed
2.5 cm (1 in) piece fresh root ginger, grated
3 teaspoons Garam Masala, see page 51
1 teaspoon cayenne pepper

Cut aubergines (eggplants) in half lengthwise and sprinkle with turmeric and salt.

Heat 75 ml (2½ fl oz/⅓ cup) oil in a large frying pan and fry aubergines (eggplants) for about 5 minutes, stirring frequently, until golden brown. Stir in garlic and ginger and fry for 2 minutes. Stir in garam masala, cayenne pepper and remaining oil and cook, uncovered, for 10-15 minutes, stirring occasionally, or until aubergines are soft.

Leave to cool, then spoon into sterilised jars. Cover jars with a dry cloth and leave in a sunny place for 3 days, stirring gently every day. Seal jars and store in a cool, dark place for up to 2 months. Serve the pickle at room temperature.

Makes about 750 g (1½ lb).

Note: If baby aubergines (eggplants) are unavailable, use larger ones and quarter lengthwise, then slice and prepare as above.

CUCUMBER RAITA

CARROT & PISTACHIO RAITA

⅓ cucumber
250 ml (8 fl oz/1 cup) natural yogurt
1 tablespoon chopped fresh coriander
1 tablespoon chopped fresh mint
1 green chilli, seeded and finely chopped
salt
1 teaspoon cumin seeds
1 teaspoon mustard seeds
coriander or mint leaves, to garnish

Cut cucumber into 0.3 cm x 1 cm (⅛ x ½ in) sticks and place in a bowl.

30 g (1 oz/¼ cup) coarsely chopped pistachio nuts
60 g (2 oz/⅓ cup) raisins
90 ml (3 fl oz/⅓ cup) boiling water
4 carrots, coarsely grated
185 ml (6 fl oz/¾ cup) natural yogurt
1 tablespoon chopped fresh mint
½ teaspoon chilli powder
½ teaspoon cardamom seeds, crushed
½ teaspoon ground cumin
salt

Put pistachio nuts and raisins in a small bowl and pour over boiling water. Leave to soak for 30 minutes, then drain and pat dry with absorbent kitchen paper.

Add yogurt, coriander, mint and chilli and stir gently to mix. Season with salt. Chill for 30 minutes.

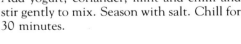

Put carrots, yogurt, chopped mint, chilli powder, cardamom seeds and cumin in a bowl, season with salt and stir to mix.

Meanwhile, put cumin and mustard seeds in a frying pan and dry roast them over a medium heat for 1-2 minutes, until they begin to pop. Leave to cool, then sprinkle over the yogurt mixture. Serve chilled, garnished with coriander or mint leaves.

Makes about 375 ml (12 fl oz/1½ cups).

Chill for 30 minutes. Stir all but 2 tablespoons pistachio nuts and raisins into yogurt, then sprinkle remainder on top. Serve the raita chilled.

Makes about 375 ml (12 fl oz/1½ cups).

Variation: Substitute chopped blanched almonds for pistachio nuts.

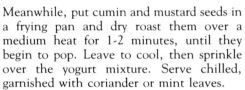

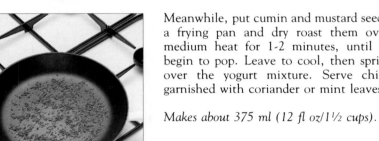

BEETROOT & YOGURT SALAD

6 cooked baby beetroots
250 ml (8 fl oz/1 cup) natural yogurt
1 teaspoon sugar
salt and cayenne pepper
1 tablespoon snipped fresh chives
small bunch of chives, to garnish

Cut beetroot into 0.3 cm (⅛ in) thick slices and arrange on a serving plate. Cover and chill for 30 minutes.

Put yogurt into a bowl and stir in sugar, then season with salt and cayenne pepper. Chill for 30 minutes.

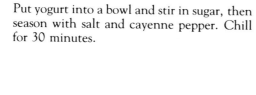

Pour yogurt mixture over beetroot and sprinkle with snipped chives. Serve chilled, garnished with chives.

Serves 4-6.

Variation: Cut beetroot into tiny dice and stir into yogurt before chilling.

CUCUMBER & CHILLIES

250 g (8 oz) cucumber
salt
2 fresh green chillies, seeded and finely sliced, see Note
1 small fresh red chilli, seeded and finely chopped
½ teaspoon onion seeds
6 teaspoons white wine vinegar
1 teaspoon caster sugar

Very thinly slice the cucumber.

Place the cucumber slices in a colander and sprinkle with plenty of salt. Leave to drain for 30 minutes, then rinse thoroughly under cold running water. Pat dry with absorbent kitchen paper and arrange on a serving plate.

In a small bowl, mix together chillies and onion seeds and sprinkle over cucumber. Put vinegar and sugar in a bowl and mix well. Sprinkle over cucumber, then cover and chill for 30 minutes. Serve chilled.

Serves 4-6.

Note: The seeds of chillies can be left in, if preferred, to make the dish very hot.

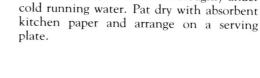

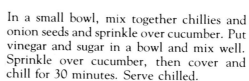

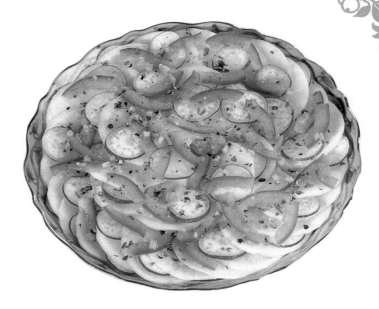

TOMATO KUCHUMBER

WHITE & RED RADISH SALAD

375 g (12 oz) cherry tomatoes
6 spring onions
1 green chilli, seeded and chopped
3 teaspoons lemon juice
2 tablespoons chopped fresh coriander
salt and cayenne pepper
spring onion tassels, to garnish, if desired

Quarter the cherry tomatoes and arrange them in a serving bowl.

185 g (6 oz) white radish (mooli)
10 red radishes
1 small green pepper (capsicum)
1 fresh green chilli, seeded and finely chopped
6 teaspoons lime juice
salt
6 black peppercorns, coarsely ground
1 tablespoon chopped fresh mint

Peel and thinly slice white radish and slice red radishes. Arrange on a serving plate.

Cut spring onions diagonally into long, thin slices. Scatter onions and chilli over tomatoes and gently mix together.

Cut pepper (capsicum) into 6 lengthwise, remove seeds and stalk and slice finely. Scatter pepper (capsicum) and chilli over radishes.

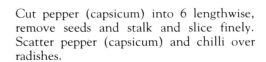

Sprinkle vegetables with lemon juice and coriander and season with salt and cayenne pepper, then cover and chill for 30 minutes. Serve chilled, garnished with spring onion tassels, if desired.

Serves 4-6.

Variation: Use larger tomatoes, if preferred: slice thinly and arrange on a serving plate. Scatter other ingredients over top before chilling.

Sprinkle salad with lime juice, salt, peppercorns and mint. Cover and chill for 30 minutes. Serve chilled.

Serves 4-6.

CHAPATI

155 g (5 oz/1¼ cups) plain flour
155 g (5 oz/1¼ cups) wholewheat flour
salt
60 g (2 oz/¼ cup) butter or ghee, melted, for serving

Sift flours and salt together into a mixing bowl and tip in any bran caught in sieve. Mix in about 185 ml (6 fl oz/¾ cup) water to make a soft dough.

Knead dough on a lightly floured surface for about 5 minutes, until smooth and pliable, then, with wet hands, knead dough for 1 minute more to make it extra smooth. Wrap in plastic wrap and chill for 30 minutes. Divide dough into 12 pieces and roll each out on a lightly floured surface to a 12.5 cm (5 in) round.

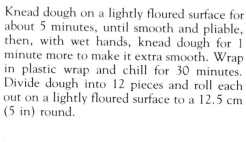

Heat a griddle or heavy-based frying pan on a medium heat and cook dough rounds, 1 at a time, floury side down, for 1-2 minutes, until beginning to bubble on surface. Turn over and cook second side for ½-1 minute, pressing with a folded dry cloth during cooking to make them puff up. Wrap each chapati in a dry cloth as soon as it is ready. Serve them warm, brushed with melted butter or ghee.

Makes 12.

NAAN

500 g (1 lb/4 cups) plain flour
1 teaspoon baking powder
½ teaspoon bicarbonate of soda
salt
1 egg, beaten
6 tablespoons natural yogurt
45 g (1½ oz/9 teaspoons) butter or ghee, melted
about 250 ml (8 fl oz/1 cup) milk
3 teaspoons poppy seeds

Sift flour, baking powder and bicarbonate of soda together into a mixing bowl. Season with salt.

Stir in egg, yogurt and 30 g (1 oz/6 teaspoons) butter or ghee. Gradually mix in enough milk to make a soft dough. Cover bowl with a damp cloth and put in a warm place for 2 hours. Preheat oven to 200C (400F/Gas 6). Knead dough on a lightly floured surface for 2-3 minutes, until smooth, then divide dough into 8 pieces.

Roll each piece into a ball, then roll out to make ovals about 15 cm (6 in) long, pulling ends to stretch dough into shape. Brush ovals with water and place wet-side down on greased baking trays. Brush dry side with melted butter or ghee and sprinkle with poppy seeds. Bake for 8-10 minutes, until puffy and golden brown. Serve at once.

Makes 8.

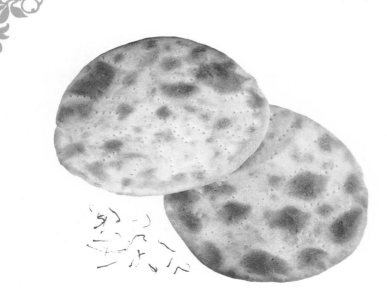

FLAKY OVEN BREAD

500 g (1 lb/4 cups) plain flour
salt
125 g (4 oz/½ cup) butter or ghee
2 teaspoons caster sugar
about 500 ml (16 fl oz/2 cups) milk
pinch saffron threads

Sift flour and salt to taste together into a mixing bowl. Rub in all but 15 g (½ oz/3 teaspoons) of the butter or ghee until mixture resembles breadcrumbs. Stir in sugar, then add about 315 ml (10 fl oz/1¼ cups) milk to make a soft dough.

Knead dough until smooth, then put in a clean, lightly oiled bowl. Cover and leave in a cool place for 2 hours. Put remaining milk in a small pan and heat until almost boiling, add saffron threads and leave to soak for 1½-2 hours. Preheat oven to 230C (450F/Gas 8) and place a heavy baking tray in oven to heat. Knead dough on a lightly floured surface and divide into 8 pieces. Roll 4 pieces at a time into balls, keeping rest covered with a dry cloth.

Flatten and roll first 4 balls out to 15 cm (6 in) rounds. Prick all over with a fork. Press onto heated baking tray in oven and bake for about 8 minutes, until beginning to brown, sprinkling rounds with a little saffron milk twice without removing them from oven. Melt remaining butter or ghee and brush over breads, then stack them buttered-sides together and wrap in a dry cloth while preparing remaining rounds. Serve warm.

Makes 8.

PARATHA

250 g (8 oz/2 cups) plain flour
250 g (8 oz/2 cups) wholewheat flour
salt
½ teaspoon onion seeds
½ teaspoon celery seeds
250 g (8 oz/1 cup) butter or ghee, melted
celery leaves, to garnish

Sift flours and salt to taste together into a mixing bowl and tip in any bran caught in the sieve. Stir in onion and celery seeds, then mix in about 155 ml (5 fl oz/⅔ cup) water to form a fairly soft dough.

Knead dough on a lightly floured surface for 5 minutes or until pliable and smooth. Wrap in plastic wrap and chill for 30 minutes. Divide dough into 10 pieces and roll each out to a 12.5 cm (5 in) round. Brush 1 side of each round with butter or ghee, then fold in half with buttered side inside. Brush top side with butter and fold in half again to make a triangle.

Roll out on a lightly floured surface until straight sides measure about 12.5 cm (5 in). Heat a griddle or heavy-based frying pan and brush with butter or ghee. Cook 2 or 3 at a time for 1 minute, then brush with butter, turn over and cook 1-2 minutes more. Stack on a plate and cover with a cloth while cooking remainder. Serve warm, garnished with celery leaves.

Makes 10.

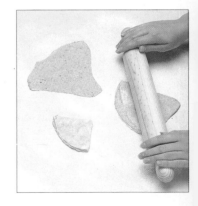

POORI

45 g (1½ oz/⅓ cup) plain flour
45 g (1½ oz/⅓ cup) wholewheat flour
pinch salt
¼ teaspoon cardamom seeds
about 2 tablespoons vegetable oil plus extra for deep frying
about 60 ml (2 fl oz/¼ cup) warm water

Sift flours and salt together into a mixing bowl and tip in any bran caught in sieve. Stir in cardamom seeds and 3 teaspoons oil and mix in enough of the water to make a soft dough.

Knead dough for 5 minutes on a lightly oiled surface with a little oil rubbed into hands to prevent them sticking until dough is soft and pliable. Cover with plastic wrap and leave to rest for 10 minutes. Divide dough into 8 pieces and roll into balls. Dust balls with flour and cover with a damp cloth. Roll each ball out to a 7.5 cm (3 in) round, keeping unrolled balls and finished rounds covered with the cloth.

Half-fill a deep-fat pan or fryer with oil and heat to 190C (375F) or until a day-old cube of bread browns in 40 seconds. Fry poori 1 at a time, turning over once, for ½-1 minute, until golden. Keep patting top of each poori gently with a slotted spoon as it cooks to make it puff up. Serve at once.

Makes 8.

DOSA

60 g (2 oz/⅓ cup) urad dhal (mung beans, split not husked)
155 g (5 oz/1 cup) long-grain rice
2 spring onions, finely chopped
2 tablespoons chopped fresh coriander
2.5 cm (1 in) piece fresh root ginger, grated
1 fresh green chilli, seeded and chopped
½ teaspoon salt
about 3 tablespoons vegetable oil
coriander leaves, to garnish

Wash dhal and rice thoroughly and put into separate bowls. Add 500 ml (16 fl oz/2 cups) water to each and leave to soak for 3 hours, then drain well.

Put dhal in a blender or food processor fitted with a metal blade. Add 90 ml (3 fl oz/⅓ cup) water and process until smooth. Purée rice with 90 ml (3 fl oz/ ⅓ cup) water in same way. Mix purées together in a large bowl, cover with a damp cloth and set aside at room temperature for about 12 hours.

Stir in onions, coriander, ginger, chilli, salt and about 9 teaspoons water to make a batter. Heat a 15 cm (6 in) frying pan, brush with a little oil, then spoon in 2-3 tablespoons batter and spread into a 10 cm (4 in) circle. Cook over a high heat for about 3 minutes, turning over with a fish slice after half the time, until browned. Cover with a dry cloth while cooking remainder. Serve warm, garnished with coriander leaves.

Makes about 12.

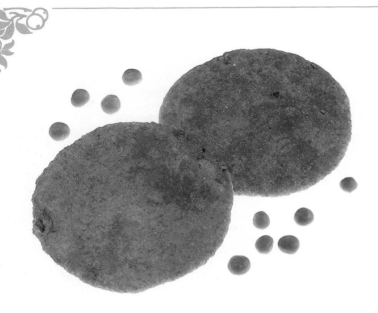

GREEN PEA KACHORI

250 g (8 oz/1¾ cups) wholewheat flour
¼ teaspoon salt
½ teaspoon cumin seeds
½ teaspoon aniseeds
6 teaspoons vegetable oil plus extra for deep frying
1 fresh green chilli, seeded and chopped
2.5 cm (1 in) piece fresh root ginger, grated
60 g (2 oz) frozen peas, thawed

Sift flour and salt together into a mixing bowl and tip in any bran caught in sieve. Mix in about 60 ml (2 fl oz/¼ cup) water to make a soft dough. Knead on a lightly floured surface for 5 minutes.

Set dough aside, covered with a dry cloth. Heat a frying pan, add cumin seeds and aniseeds and dry fry for ½-1 minute, until beginning to pop, then grind with a mortar and pestle. Heat oil in pan, add ground spices, chilli and ginger and fry for 2 minutes. Mash peas, then add to pan and cook for 1 minute more. Leave to cool, then divide dough into 12 pieces and roll into balls.

Make a depression in each dough ball, press in about 1 teaspoon filling and smooth over dough to seal. Roll each ball out on a lightly floured surface to a 7.5 cm (3 in) round. Half-fill a deep-fat pan or fryer with oil and heat to 190C (375F) or until a cube of day-old bread browns in 40 seconds. Fry 2 kachori at a time for 2-3 minutes or until golden brown. Serve warm.

Makes 12.

NIMKI

125 g (4 oz/1 cup) plain flour
½ teaspoon salt
15 g (½ oz/3 teaspoons) butter or ghee
large pinch chilli powder
¼ teaspoon caster sugar
½ teaspoon onion seeds
vegetable oil for deep frying
chilli flowers, to garnish, if desired

Sift flour and salt together into a mixing bowl, then rub in butter or ghee until mixture resembles breadcrumbs.

Stir in chilli powder, caster sugar and onion seeds, then mix in about 60 ml (2 fl oz/¼ cup) water to make a soft dough. Roll out dough on a floured surface to a thickness of 0.3 cm (⅛ in). Prick all over with a fork and cut into 2.5 cm (1 in) strips. Cut strips diagonally to make about 30 diamond shapes.

Half-fill a deep-fat pan or fryer with oil and heat to 190C (375F) or until a cube of day-old bread browns in 40 seconds. Fry nimki in 2 or 3 batches for 1-2 minutes each, until crisp and golden brown. Drain well and cool. Serve garnished with chilli flowers, if desired.

Makes about 30.

Note: These tiny crisp breads are ideal for party nibbles. Make 2 days ahead and store in an airtight tin.

ORANGE SHERBET

about 8 oranges
125 g (4 oz/½ cup) caster sugar
ice cubes
625 ml (20 fl oz/2½ cups) sparkling mineral water
orange peel spirals and mint sprigs, to decorate

Squeeze juice from oranges to make 625 ml (20 fl oz/2½ cups) juice.

Meanwhile, put sugar and 625 ml (20 fl oz/2½ cups) water in a large saucepan and cook over a low heat, stirring occasionally, until sugar has dissolved. Bring to the boil and boil gently, uncovered, for 5 minutes. Add orange juice and boil gently for a further 5 minutes. Leave to cool, then chill.

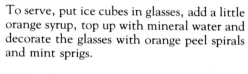

To serve, put ice cubes in glasses, add a little orange syrup, top up with mineral water and decorate the glasses with orange peel spirals and mint sprigs.

Makes about 1.2 litres (2 pints/5 cups).

Note: Use ready-made freshly squeezed orange juice, if preferred.

MILK & SAFFRON SHERBET

½ teaspoon saffron threads
6 teaspoons boiling water
90 g (3 oz/¾ cup) shelled pistachio nuts
seeds from 10 green cardamom pods
60 g (2 oz/¼ cup) caster sugar
1.2 litres (2 pints/5 cups) cold milk
crushed ice

Put saffron and boiling water in a small bowl and leave to soak for 30 minutes.

Put saffron and water in a blender or food processor with two-thirds pistachio nuts, cardamom seeds and sugar. Process until smooth. Add milk and process until frothy. Chop remaining nuts.

Half-fill glasses with ice and pour in frothy milk. Sprinkle with remaining pistachio nuts and serve at once.

Makes about 1.2 litres (2 pints/5 cups).

FRAGRANT LEMON SHERBET

SPICED TEA

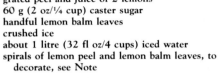 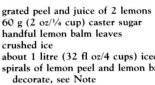

grated peel and juice of 2 lemons
60 g (2 oz/¼ cup) caster sugar
handful lemon balm leaves
crushed ice
about 1 litre (32 fl oz/4 cups) iced water
spirals of lemon peel and lemon balm leaves, to
    decorate, see Note

5 teaspoons black peppercorns
3 teaspoons cardamom seeds
3 teaspoons cloves
4 cm (1½ in) cinnamon stick
30 g (1 oz/⅓ cup) ground ginger
Indian tea leaves
boiling water
sugar and milk, to taste

Put lemon peel and juice, sugar and lemon balm leaves in a blender or food processor and process until smooth. Strain into a jug and chill.

Put peppercorns, cardamom seeds, cloves and cinnamon in a mortar and grind to a fine powder with a pestle. Add ginger and grind again for a few seconds to mix.

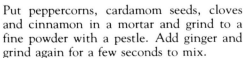 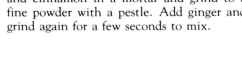

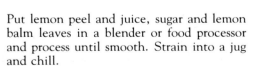

Fill glasses with crushed ice, pour over a little lemon concentrate and top up with iced water. Serve, decorated with spirals of lemon peel and lemon balm leaves.

Makes about 1.2 litres (2 pints/5 cups).

Note: To make lemon spiral decoration, cut a long strip of peel using a cannelle knife. Wind round a skewer or chopstick, fasten securely and blanch in boiling water for a few seconds. Rinse in cold water and remove skewer or chopstick.

Make a pot of tea and add about ½ tablespoon of spice mixture and leave in a warm place for 1-2 minutes to brew. Serve hot, with sugar and milk.

Makes about 8 tablespoons spice mix, enough for 16 pots tea.

Note: Store remaining spice mixture in a screw-topped jar in a dark cupboard to preserve its flavour. It will keep for 2-3 months.

LIME & MINT SHERBET

INDIAN SUMMER PUNCH

4-6 limes
60 g (2 oz/¼ cup) caster sugar
pinch salt
handful mint leaves
ice cubes
about 1 litre (32 fl oz/4 cups) iced water
mint leaves and lime slices, to decorate

Squeeze enough limes to make 90 ml (3 fl oz/ ⅓ cup) juice.

3 teaspoons fennel seeds
seeds from 6 green cardamom pods
3 cloves
4 black peppercorns
60 g (2 oz/½ cup) ground almonds
30 g (1 oz/¼ cup) shelled pistachio nuts
60 g (2 oz/½ cup) sunflower seeds
315 ml (10 fl oz/1¼ cups) boiling water
125 g (4 oz/½ cup) caster sugar
940 ml (30 fl oz/3¾ cups) cold milk
apple slices and fennel sprigs, to decorate

Put fennel and cardamom seeds, cloves and peppercorns in a mortar and grind to a fine powder with a pestle.

Put the juice in a blender or food processor fitted with a metal blade. Add sugar, salt and mint leaves and process until smooth. Strain into a jug, then chill.

Put almonds, pistachios and sunflower seeds in a small bowl and pour over 90 ml (3 fl oz/ ⅓ cup) boiling water. Leave to soak for 20 minutes, then drain. Put in a blender or food processor fitted with a metal blade and add remaining water and process until smooth.

Half-fill tall glasses with ice cubes, add a little lime juice concentrate and top up with iced water. Serve at once, decorated with mint leaves and lime slices.

Makes about 1.2 litres (2 pints/5 cups).

Add spices and sugar and process again. Strain through a cloth or 2 layers of muslin, squeezing paste to extract as much liquid as possible. Discard paste and chill liquid for at least 1 hour, then mix with milk. Serve in tall glasses over ice, decorated with apple slices and fennel sprigs.

Makes about 1.9 litres (3 pints/7½ cups).

Note: If preferred, grind spices in a coffee grinder.

INDEX